P
Career Choices in M
Musical and Psychological Perspectives

"This is a definitive study that is a must-read for musicians young and old as well as general readers interested in the music profession. Julie Jaffee Nagel's carefully researched work combines the perceptions of a musician and psychologist dealing with post-pandemic challenges involving musicians' contributions to our society."
—**Joseph W. Polisi, president emeritus, The Juilliard School**

"I do not wish to rob glory from a student's hopefulness, but rather, I want them to know that the very hard work will somehow pay off. Each individual will have their own brave story to tell. This much-needed book by Nagel provides important and continual support."
—**Ruth Slenczynska, concert pianist**

"As a practicing musician and psychoanalyst, Nagel is well-suited and uniquely qualified to help us understand and process the traumatic effects of the global pandemic on career choices faced by musicians. This timely reflection with its optimistic outlook weaves a compelling narrative using real-life examples, many of them her own, along with psychological concepts to provide a framework upon which to build or rebuild a successful music career. It should be required reading for everyone who is contemplating or is currently engaged in the music profession."
—**Gary Ingle, executive director and CEO, Music Teachers National Association (MTNA)**

"This book offers deep psychological insights and a wealth of information on everything from early childhood experience, stage fright, concert fees, and so much more. It's a veritable handbook of advice guiding musicians at every level into the new and ever-changing world of music."
—**Arnold Steinhardt, first violin, Guarneri String Quartet**

"Nagel knows the field as a trained musical performer and a practicing clinician who is an international authority on work inhibition and performance block. There is none better!"
—**Peter Loewenberg, professor emeritus, history and political psychology, University of California, Los Angeles**

"This book is especially appropriate and perfectly timed, given the tremendous challenges artists have been facing for the past few years. Nagel promotes a thoughtful and holistic approach to helping the reader make wise and appropriate decisions for the future. Her book will encourage constructive personal introspection."
—Gail Berenson, professor emerita of piano, Ohio University; former president, MTNA

"Nagel, uniquely qualified to combine psychoanalysis and music, offers a design for a meaningful life as a musician. Mining the wealth of her personal and professional experience, she addresses both the economic demands and the many rewards of commitment to music."
—Sandra G. Hershberg, training and supervising analyst, Institute for Contemporary Psychotherapy and Psychoanalysis, Washington, DC

"For years, music students (and their parents) have questioned the financial viability of pursuing music as a career. The pandemic only added to concerns. Nagel discusses these issues from psychological development and emotional health to practical issues of making money as a musician in today's world. This is a must-read for every music student and professors who work with them."
—E. L. Lancaster, piano faculty, California State University, Northridge

"A must-read for any musician engaged in or considering a career in music. Nagel provides valuable insight into essential but rarely discussed subjects that impact the lives of every professional musician."
—John Viscardi, opera singer; co-founder of ArtSmart

"Nagel addresses the issues that every musician faces in their careers. She explores them from personal and research-oriented perspectives while challenging students to examine their reasons for pursuing a career in music. With her background in music and psychology, there is no one more qualified than her to examine these issues."
—Gayle Kowalchyk, piano faculty, California State University, Northridge

"This is an essential guide for musicians and music teachers—really for every teacher in every discipline. Nagel helps with the difficult, conflicting career choices we must make throughout our lifetimes, preparing all students and teachers for the dangerous temptations that arise."
—Stanley J. Coen, clinical professor of psychiatry, Columbia University; training and supervising analyst, Columbia University Center for Psychoanalytic Training and Research

"Nagel's psychological insights make this book a must-read. Her chapters on the 'Pursuit of Perfection' and 'The Golden Allure of Celebrity' should be read by anyone contemplating a rabbinic career."
—**Rabbi Bruce Warshal, pulpit rabbi and lawyer; economics instructor, Miami University of Ohio**

"This is a unique and important book. Nagel deftly uses psychology to identify the basis of our career choices and their impact on identity and self-esteem. With vivid case examples, she highlights the musician's emotional struggle for success. Above all, this book reminds us that music and musicians inspire and sustain us."
—**Stefan A. Pasternack, faculty, Florida Psychoanalytic Center; affiliate professor, Florida Atlantic University**

Career Choices in Music
beyond the Pandemic

Career Choices in Music beyond the Pandemic

Musical and Psychological Perspectives

Julie Jaffee Nagel

ROWMAN & LITTLEFIELD
Lanham • Boulder • New York • London

Published by Rowman & Littlefield
An imprint of The Rowman & Littlefield Publishing Group, Inc.
4501 Forbes Boulevard, Suite 200, Lanham, Maryland 20706
www.rowman.com

86-90 Paul Street, London EC2A 4NE

British Library Cataloguing in Publication Information Available

Library of Congress Cataloging-in-Publication Data

Names: Nagel, Julie Jaffee, author.
Title: Career choices in music beyond the pandemic : musical and
    psychological perspectives / Julie Jaffee Nagel.
Description: Lanham : Rowman & Littlefield Publishers, 2023. | Includes
    bibliographical references and index.
Identifiers: LCCN 2022046984 (print) | LCCN 2022046985 (ebook) | ISBN
    9781538168387 (cloth) | ISBN 9781538168394 (paperback) | ISBN
    9781538168400 (epub)
Subjects: LCSH: Musicians—Psychology. | Psychoanalysis and music. |
    Music—Psychological aspects. | COVID-19 Pandemic, 2020—-Psychological
    aspects. | COVID-19 Pandemic, 2020—-Economic aspects.
Classification: LCC ML3830 .N3324 2023 (print) | LCC ML3830 (ebook) | DDC
    781.1/1—dcundefined
LC record available at https://lccn.loc.gov/2022046984
LC ebook record available at https://lccn.loc.gov/2022046985

♾️™ The paper used in this publication meets the minimum requirements of
American National Standard for Information Sciences—Permanence of Paper
for Printed Library Materials, ANSI/NISO Z39.48-1992.

Contents

~

Prelude

Career choice is one of the most important decisions we make in our life-time. *Career Choices in Music beyond the Pandemic: Musical and Psychological Perspectives* explores how your work, your personal identity, and a variety of feelings and actions are linked importantly to your choice of a career in music. Galvanized by the ravages of the pandemic, I felt a need to write about career "choice," which turned into choices to include at least two realities: 1) that the compensation of a musician typically necessitates working at more than one job (often outside music) and 2) that the pandemic cast a light on the necessity of rethinking, rebuilding, and possibly redesigning our concept of careers in the arts. Rather than succumbing to the understandable despair that accompanied COVID-19's unwelcome and sudden descent into our lives and careers, we should recognize how this trauma has energized and actually ex-panded choices for rewarding and creative work in a music career of the future.

The idea of writing *Career Choices in Music beyond the Pandemic* entered my mental radar when I, like numerous others, was feeling overwhelmed by the pandemic. I felt a need to overcome my sense of helplessness and also to pause and think about the musical influences that led me to pursue a career in music and—years later—to blend it with psychology and psy-choanalysis. All of us have been upended by the pandemic and have been forced to make unexpected decisions about our work. It is my conviction that the musician's work beyond the pandemic will thrive long past the taming of COVID-19. Musicians already have demonstrated that they are an integral part of the healing process.

This book recognizes that music performance is a kind of labor. We become enchanted as we listen and watch musicians *play* concerts. Yet *play* for the musician is hard *work*; many hours are spent offstage preparing for what we hear and see in public that appears effortless and playful.

Work is uniquely personal for musicians who begin music lessons in childhood. I offer the suggestion that a music career chooses the musician—unknowingly, at a very young age, making sounds in the nursery is the baby's music just as play is serious work for a young child. When they pursue serious professional training, musicians graduate into a job market where, statistically speaking, the supply of talented individuals far exceeds available employment opportunities. Both working and not working become powerfully linked with the musician's sense of "self."

When I wrote this book, it was challenging as well as consolidating for me to reflect backward and look forward beyond career decisions I made (often unknowingly at the time) that eventually blended my career in music and added additional years of training in psychology, social work, and psychoanalysis. The adventure has brought rigorous challenges, sacrifices, and deep pleasure. My personal expedition provides a backdrop and a subtext which informs each chapter, helping to illustrate the various rewards, challenges, and decisions that await musicians.

After I graduated from Juilliard, my career was solidly planted in music: Over the course of approximately fourteen years, I gave private piano lessons, taught general music in public schools, and taught piano during the summers at the National Music Camp in Interlochen, Michigan, in addition to performing. But my music ambitions took an unexpected turn. This evolved, at least consciously, around my lifelong experience with stage fright. Over time I realized that career choice in music involved so much more than performing and teaching. Clearly, practicing harder or longer did not provide emotional security onstage. At that time, almost no one spoke or wrote about stage fright as it pertained to music performance. It was perceived as a stigma or lack of talent, yet it was, and still often remains, an "elephant in the room" (personal communication, pianist Leon Fleisher). I returned to graduate school to major in psychology and social work at the University of Michigan. Not long after earning my PhD in both areas, my interest in motivation about careers in music led me to complete psychoanalytic training at the Michigan Psychoanalytic Institute. Redirection of my original musical goals deepened, and over the years I have rewritten my personal script about my original career choice.

In my clinical work over many years, I have worked with musicians and nonmusicians to better understand why they do not appreciate their strengths which become buried beneath painful anxiety, masked by diminished self-confidence, and concealed by low self-esteem. I have seen people rework painful attitudes and habits and discovered why and how personal and professional aspirations can become satisfying goals. I hope reading this book will help you appreciate who you "are" and value what you have to share through your musical talent.

My interest in the musician's career choice has raised many questions. Why do people pursue a career in work as demanding as music, which offers low economic compensation, intense competition, frequent rejection, and an oversupply of talent for available jobs? What are some psychological factors that draw some individuals to pursue a career in music? Why does music evoke powerful feelings? How does music do this? What is the musician's contribution to society and mental health? Why is there a stigma about experiencing performance anxiety and seeking treatment for it? What are some of the nonmusical challenges in a music career that lead some musicians to deviate from teaching and act out personal problems with their students in their careers? What are the power and value of music both in mental life and in the world community? What are the opportunities and challenges for the music performers and teachers before, during, and beyond the pandemic? How can musicians become artistic and social ambassadors and teachers beyond the classroom, studio, and concert hall? The pandemic has closed many doors but also opened numerous other possibilities for gratifying work in music. Clearly, a career in music is more than a job and includes many contrapuntal themes both onstage and offstage.

Career Choices in Music beyond the Pandemic is a psychological and musical journey that will raise more questions than it answers. I do not offer a model for choosing a career, nor is this book intended as a platform to provide one-size-fits-all advice. I hope it will motivate you to think about your professional and personal goals and pose some questions of your own. One key question is What is the role of music in the composition of our unique life stories from the blueprint of genetics and the influences of psychological and societal factors? I took two roads (music and mind) that have come together but ostensibly also diverged from my original choice (to liberally paraphrase poet Robert Frost), which, for me, has made all the difference.[1]

The demands of our momentous career choices, knowingly and unknowingly, are perhaps more complex now than before COVID-19. Yet in many ways, choices about working in music are more straightforward than they were pre-pandemic. Musicians must become part of society rather than only perform from stages. Musicians must play significant roles in teaching and interacting with audiences in the community in novel venues rather than flying into town, playing a concert, and rushing back to the airport to travel to another gig or, perhaps, less glamorously, performing locally and returning the next morning to a nonmusic job to earn a living.

Working on this book during this unsettling time generated many feelings and memories for me. At times I felt stuck, frightened, and overwhelmed by the pandemic's threats to society and to physical and mental health. Thinking about career choices (plural) in music gave me reassurance about options, creativity, and continuity. Writing this book has refreshed my optimism and enthusiasm about pursuing a career in music.

Musicians' gifts, which include resilience and discipline and their intrinsic artistic, personal, and social value, will continue to be expressed through their ingenuity and talent in the days and years ahead. Musicians provide an aural antidote in society to the trauma of the pandemic. Music, reciprocally, can provide healing for the musicians as well. I cannot imagine my life without music that has become interfaced with psychology and psychoanalysis expressed in my thinking and work. This book reflects my profound respect for all musicians who teach, study, and perform. Artistic imagination is unlimited and ready to be expressed creatively during formidable circumstances. These circumstances are now.

Chapter 1 invites you to think about what influenced you to choose music as your career choice. Through data, personal reflections, and clinical accounts, multiple issues that influence a career choice in music are discussed. Emphasis is placed on some of the psychological implications involved in seeking, perhaps losing, and creatively redesigning a career that was upended—whether gradually or suddenly—following the thunderbolt of the pandemic.

Chapter 2 considers the economics of the music profession. Musicians (particularly those who are not "stars") often work for lower-than-average wages. This is inverse to the years of intense preparation required to pursue a career in music, which begins in childhood. COVID-19's abruptly forced cancellation of concerts, closure of music venues, shuttering of schools, and halting of private lessons meant the elimination of income earned from performing or teaching. Equally important, the disappearance of live music in our social and culturally-locked-down lives deprived the public of innumerable personal interactions and satisfactions gained from sharing music with others at in-person events. In addition to coping with anxiety, depression, loss, uncertainty, fear of the unknown, illness, rising death rates, and unseen grief, musicians have suffered economic losses that deeply impacted a future that was already difficult and unpredictable. Data from the National Endowment for the Arts and other pertinent research about musicians' earnings illustrate the dramatic financial impact of the lockdown on musicians and the ensuing emotional trauma that cast a dark shadow on the entire music profession, indeed upon so many people worldwide.

Chapter 3 illustrates a model of human psychological, social, and biological development to consider occupational choice as a cornerstone of our senses of ourselves, i.e., our personal identities. Occupational and musical development occur over a lifetime and both reflect who we "are" and what we "do." The human life cycle from birth to death provides an anchor for this discussion, as does my belief that music begins in the nursery. As we develop, some children acquire a fascination with making music that evolves into a decision, during late adolescence and young adulthood, to pursue music professionally. Challenges, rewards, disappointments, and successes that evolve are discussed over the course of the eight stages in the life cycle that are defined by psychologist and educator Erik Erikson based on his classic work *Childhood and Society*.[2]

Chapter 4 deepens our thinking about money as it explores an interface of the psychological meaning of money and the identity of the musician. The chapter emphasizes the financial value that society places on the arts when thinking about money and the musician. Exploring this complex topic also includes examining some of the psychological factors that are embedded in the musician's sense of self that allow talented people to work for less income than their talent and work prepare them to do. What are some of the underlying dynamic factors involving money that are brought by the musician to the profession, and what are the issues within the music profession itself that lead to income discrepancies affecting musicians? What are some of the economic challenges that await the musician emerging from the pandemic that can impact positively on earning an appropriate and reliable income commensurate with talent, demands of the profession, and the musician's self-image? How does one value earning tangible dollars as well as what I call "psychic income"?[3] These questions are posed both to musicians and to society. If addressed, they have the potential to bring positive change to career choices (plural) in music. A deeper understanding about money can inform both earning potential and psychological health.

Chapter 5 presents original research findings regarding career choice among four specific categories of musicians. Deriving from quantitative and qualitative methodology as defined in the Identity Status Interview constructed by James Marcia, these data suggest various personality characteristics of some individuals who consider or choose a career in music.[4]

Chapter 6 addresses the illusion and disillusionment that is felt by so many musicians who insist that nothing less than "perfection" will bring success. Typically, disillusionment ensues when a wish-fantasy is not realized or feels beyond reach. The alternative of accepting who we "are" rather than who we "are not" leads to the realization that a belief in one's capabilities leads to increased self-regard to replace dwelling on the impossibility of achieving flawlessness.

Chapter 7 is a story within a story that, like contrapuntal music, has many interactive themes. The public's fascination with famous people is discussed, and an experience with a celebrity musician shared by a colleague and me is described and analyzed. The multiple implications, feelings, and thoughts that this experience raised include a psychological examination of how fascination with a celebrity—or a music teacher who is perceived as a "celebrity"—has the potential to evolve into what has been called the #MeToo movement. The multifaceted lessons we can learn from the examination of our own deeper motives are discussed. The chapter takes us back and forth from a real-life situation to psychological theory about what can happen when the allure of the golden celebrity and teachers can tempt some people to reach beyond accepted boundaries.

Chapter 8 explores music education—past, present, and future. Some ideas, while offered with an undercurrent of irony, underscore very serious questions for instituting some realistic, creative music and psychological concepts for educating musicians in the twenty-first century. Emphasis is placed upon helping music students and graduates, teachers, and performers think creatively about expanding career options beyond the teaching studio and concert hall that can "work" and can provide meaningful work.

Chapter 9, the final chapter, emphasizes the importance and necessity of the musician's expanded contributions in a post-pandemic world. The musician is a cultural ambassador and a teaching-performing artist who can work in communities beyond the concert stage and teaching studio. Musicians can share widely the value of music in our lives, in society, in our mental and physical health, and in culture. If music is indeed a calling, musicians are being called upon now to teach, play, and act.

A final note: I chose the cover of this book to visually represent the eventual fading of the darkness of the pandemic with the sun rising into a clear blue sky full of new opportunities. I have optimism that musicians will rise beyond the challenges of the pandemic as they make innovative and important career choices. *Career Choices in Music beyond the Pandemic: Musical and Psychological Perspectives* expresses my deep belief that an expanded view of sharing music with others beyond the concert hall and beyond the teaching studio will provide intrinsic and extrinsic rewards for musicians who have the potential to be cultural ambassadors in society and advocates for mental health as well as local and global problems. As such, music and musicians will enhance the quality of life for themselves and for countless others. Like the sunshine, musicians will rise to the challenges and opportunities beyond the pandemic.

Notes

1. Robert Frost, "The Road Not Taken," in *The Poetry of Robert Frost*, ed. Edward Connery and Lawrence Thompson (New York: Holt, Rinehart and Winston, Inc., 1972).

2. E. Erikson, *Childhood and Society* (New York: W. W. Norton & Company, 1950).

3. W. Baumol and W. Bowen, *The Performing Arts: An Economic Dilemma* (Cambridge: The M.I.T. Press, 1968).

4. J. E. Marcia, "Development and validation of ego-identity status," *Journal of Personality and Social Psychology* 3 (1966): 551–58.

~

Acknowledgments

Writing this book has allowed me to explore a topic that has fascinated me for most of my life. I was surprised not long ago when a friend (who was an archivist for my high school) sent me an English composition that he discovered when going through some old boxes. It was a paper I wrote in eleventh grade titled "Music: The Most Beautiful Language." The seeds that had been planted in my mind many years ago had already begun to take root.

In thinking about the years in my past and imagining the future years *beyond* the pandemic, I have revisited my musical roots that preceded and followed eleventh grade. Never in my most vivid dreams and wildest imagination could I have imagined the pandemic that has shaped our lives, and specifically our music careers, so relentlessly over the past two and a half years (as of this writing). Never did it enter my fantasies that I would combine my music career with psychology and psychoanalysis. Yet the unimaginable happened and has enriched my life. It is impossible to deeply thank all the people who have been part of my journey and continue to influence my work. I wish I could name everyone who has been an important link from then to now. Doing so would fill the pages here and not leave room for the content of my book.

My first piano lessons began when I was six years old with Martha Angelucci, a kind teacher with whom I studied for five years. I remember my first memory slip occurred in her studio. I was making a recording of a piece that I had composed. I felt mortified that I forgot my own music. I do not recall anyone talking with me about my feelings. I have never forgotten that experience. My need for advanced instruction became evident and was enthusiastically recommended by pianist Ruth Slenczynska, for whom I played following a concert she gave in my hometown. After her life-changing suggestion when I was eleven years old, my mother found a professor of piano at William and Mary College, Stephen Paledes. I studied with him until I left home for Juilliard after high school graduation to pursue my dream in music. He assigned appropriate repertoire and prepared me for my entrance piano audition at Juilliard. During high school, Jerry Lowder, director of the chorus for which I provided piano accompaniment, immersed me in rudimentary music theory. This allowed me to begin Juilliard with some basic concepts and feel less green than I did when arriving and enrolling in the first-year course of a four-year sequence on the literature and materials of music. Jerry Lowder also advised me to "keep your options open." At first I thought that meant he did not think I would be successful in music. Little did I realize at the time how wise his words were, predicting the need to be flexible and recognizing that I was capable, *not* unqualified, to forge my way in a notoriously difficult career in music.

My admiration and love are expressed for my Juilliard piano teacher, Josef Raieff, who expanded and deepened my piano skills and musical knowledge during the time I earned two degrees with him. His warmth as well as his belief in my ability to express myself at the piano are cornerstones of my career that turned out very differently than either of us imagined.

Many years after Juilliard, my life was enhanced by my psychology, social work, and psychoanalytic mentors, teachers, and advisors at the University of Michigan. These included Jesse Gordon, my doctoral advisor and dissertation cochair (who sensitized me to the invaluable importance of communicating "why people should care" about music or psychological and social issues); Edward Bordin, my dissertation cochair (who emphasized that careers and jobs meant a great deal more than "work"); and George Rosenwald, professor of psychology (who encouraged me with his comment "You have more to say"). My clinical supervision at the Michigan Psychoanalytic Institute included a meaningful collaboration with Channing Lipson, who offered creative and sensitive comments on my work with my patients but who always encouraged and respected my ideas "because you are in the room with the patient." Harvey Falit was an encouraging supervisor of my clinical cases. I have valued a warm, supportive, and ongoing association with my colleagues at the American Psychoanalytic Association. This is particularly true of Carolyn Gatto, Scientific Program and Meetings Director, and psychoanalysts Glen Gabbard, Salman Akhtar, Stanley Coen, Melvin Lansky, and Peter Loewenberg, who individually and all together encouraged my passion for interdisciplinary and creative work blending music and psychoanalysis. My psychoanalytic mentor and subsequently my dear friend, the late Stuart Feder, was my role model for thinking about music itself as psychoanalytic data. When I told him that I wanted to write about Mozart but thought everything had already been written about this famous composer, Stuart looked at me and replied, "Don't be so sure." This led to me writing *Conversation between Mozart and Freud*, performed in New York weeks before the COVID-19 lockdown. The late Pinchas Noy shared his important contributions about interdisciplinary perspectives between music and psychoanalysis in our interactions that occurred over years online between Israel and the US—we never met in person. Roy Schafer became a friend late in his life and shared insights and an analytic attitude about our work, although we also chatted about baseball during our visits. Stefan Pasternak, director of the Ernst and Gertrude Ticho Foundation, brought wisdom and warmth to our numerous personal conversations and committee work. I am honored to be an awardee of the Ernst and Gertrude Ticho Award and subsequently to collaborate with Stefan as the chair of the Ticho Committee. I am deeply appreciative of the Ticho Foundation's ongoing support of my work. Sunil Iyengar, director of research and analysis at the National Endowment for the Arts (NEA), and Bonnie Nichols, operations research analyst at the NEA, generously shared data about the economics of the arts during the pandemic. Special applause to Joseph Polisi, president emeritus of Juilliard, whose work on the value of the arts and music in society deeply enhanced my own thinking and who has encouraged my interdisciplinary approach. Carol Siegel, immediate past director of the Freud Museum, which is housed in Freud's last home in London, added considerable confirmation to my work, particularly regarding my *Conversation between Mozart and Freud*. She traveled from London to New York to introduce my production at Steinway Hall and graciously invited the audience to visit Freud's home. All of these colleagues and many, many others encouraged me to think creatively and reach outside the box as I began to blend psychology, psychoanalysis, and music to speak and write through my own voice.

Many friends have felt like family to me. I am deeply appreciative of my very special psychoanalytic colleague and dear friend Sandra Hershberg for her warmth, exquisite sensitivity, and insights and James Zwiebel, who often shared interesting recordings and articles about music and the arts with me. Gina Atkinson was editor of my first book, *Melodies of the Mind*, and our friendship deepened from that collaboration. My Michigan analytic colleague Charles Burch and social work colleague Susan Hildebrandt Burch have shared their love for music and analytic insights as we enjoyed dinners and lively conversations on many occasions. My long friendships with Ellen Fivenson,

Gloria and Joseph Gurt, Linda Grekin, and Bruce Warshal witnessed firsthand pre- and post-career challenges and changes—they were "in the room where (and when) it happened." I feel fortunate to call them my dear friends.

The emphasis placed upon the emotional life and education of musicians has been supported by the Music Teachers National Association (MTNA). Their awareness of the importance of mental health in working with musicians has been encouraged by CEO and Executive Director Gary Ingle and COO Brian Shepard, who have invited me to present at many national MTNA conferences. Gail Berenson, past president of MTNA, has been a good friend and collaborator; we cochaired interdisciplinary wellness programs from 1991 to 1993. I was honored to receive the Award for Distinguished Service from the National Conference on Keyboard Pedagogy in 2021. I also am appreciative of receiving the Nathan Segel Award (twice) from the Michigan Psychoanalytic Institute for my writing as well as the Karl Menninger Award from the American Psychoanalytic Association. It was an honor to chair the program Psychoanalytic Perspectives on Music at the American Psychoanalytic Association for fourteen years, which allowed me to bring together musicians and clinicians such as violinist Arnold Steinhardt and late analyst Leo Rangell. This opportunity continually refreshed my interest in writing about the pleasures and advantages of working with others beyond the consulting room and has deeply informed my thinking.

While music careers and mental health encompass much more than stage fright, I have found that this topic is of significant interest locally, nationally, and worldwide. I have been invited to present on performance anxiety, oppression, injustice as heard in music, #MeToo and music education, the value of music in mental life, and careers in music, and I had the opportunity to speak in London, France, Italy, Israel, Australia, Russia, and the British Virgin Islands as well as to be a guest presenter at universities and music organizations in the United States. I have been enriched from interacting with individuals in a variety of venues and cultures who have different experiences and backgrounds from my own.

It has been a pleasure to work with two talented editors, both of who add music and arts backgrounds to their editorial skills. Michael Tan, music acquisitions editor at Rowman and Littlefield, invited me to write on the topic of this book, which is very close to my heart and embedded in my personal and professional experience. His excellent ideas, thoughtful replies to all my questions, and collaboration throughout this project have made working together an outstanding experience. Having collaborated with Lucas McGranahan as my editor on two articles that blend psychoanalytic ideas and music recently published in The American Psychoanalyst, I did not hesitate to ask him for his editorial expertise to help keep focus and stay on track with my multifaceted topic. In an early Zoom conversation, I happened to mention a musical interval, the tritone (not a household word but a specific musical concept and sound connoting sonic ambiguity that is seeking tonal resolution that I had discussed in *West Side Story*). Lucas picked up his guitar, perched nearby, and played the tritone passage I mentioned. At that moment, I had no doubt that he would unambiguously understand my writing. I was right.

I cannot begin to count the number of piano students I have taught privately over many years, at the National Music Camp in Interlochen, Michigan, and in general music classes in public schools. I have been fortunate to be a part of the lives of a wide variety of musicians and patients whom I have seen in my teaching and clinical work. I have tremendous respect for the many people who have confronted their fears and anxieties and have trusted me.

My feline companions Aria and Steinway, five-year-old siblings, compete to sit in the chair next to me when I write. I find comfort in their gentle presence.

My psychoanalyst, the late Peter Blos Jr., MD, interacted with me in ways that allowed me to discover and explore childhood losses and adjustments, find new interests, reexamine old ideas, experience my feelings, understand myself more deeply, and think, feel, and work creatively. I will always value his sincerity, kindness, steadfastness, honesty, and deep humanity. His presence in my life continues to be a nourishing gift.

I recall that in one particular analytic session with Dr. Blos, I became flooded with thoughts and feelings. I commented, "I wish I could say at once everything that is in my mind like a full orchestra can play all the notes at the same time. I can only speak one word at a time."

I wish now that I could write to sound like a full orchestra to communicate through music everything that is in my mind about my family. Often I have written about how music evokes emotions and expresses feelings that words cannot articulate. Words, again, will have to suffice. Although I enjoy a wide variety of music, when I am asked to name my "favorite" composition (impossible—depends on what I am listening to), I return to the Rachmaninoff Third Piano Concerto (Vladimir Horowitz, pianist, and Eugene Ormandy, conductor, Philadelphia Orchestra) as my desert-island piece (and performance). The exquisite communication among composer, pianist, orchestra, and myself awakens my deepest feelings as this concerto evokes, beyond words, my affection for Louie, my husband, Sonya, our daughter, David, our son-in-law, and Sarah and Rachel, our granddaughters. Their patience with my preoccupation with the musician's occupation has been invaluable. This music also evokes cherished memories of my late mother, Elizabeth, and my grandparents, Esther and Julian. I dedicate the melodies in my mind to all of them.

CHAPTER ONE

Work

Like a song that lodges in your head, the idea for this book came to me and would not go away. I had no (conscious) intention of writing another book until I found myself writing this one. I have been a professional in music since my Juilliard graduation. Yet shortly after my Juilliard graduation, I found myself wandering in the career desert, feeling lost as to where my years of dedication to music and my music education would lead me.

I believe music chooses those who train seriously for a career in music performance and teaching. I feel that this book chose me to write it. At the time I began the book, we were in the midst of a seemingly unending pandemic. COVID-19 continues to hover overhead and new variants emerge like variations on a theme of illness that perpetuate it. Life in lockdown changed life as we knew it. Musicians were severely affected when performances were canceled suddenly and their income, typically inappropriately low to compensate or reward them for years of rigorous training, dropped below the poverty level or disappeared altogether.

Politically, we face elections that can decide the future and the price of freedom for years to come. Anger and lack of direction that affect the body and mind are rampant worldwide: As I write this, just yesterday a senseless shooting killed nineteen young students and two teachers in an elementary school in Uvalde, Texas, which fills me with grief, feeling a need to "do something." The years of racial oppression, gun control failures, economic crises, environmental challenges, the war in Ukraine, and political upheaval like many of us have never experienced are blaring counterpoint to the story of musicians and their career choices in which classical performers and college and private teachers aspire to work and inspire others through making and teaching music. My need to "do something" presents itself as me contributing to the idea that the value of music in mental life is necessary and can be healing. Music touches many people in ways that they find soothing or energizing or as accompaniment for mourning or celebrating. Since my career in music has modulated to my work as a psychologist and psychoanalyst and not the performer I set out to be, I needed to write *now*.

There are joys and difficult challenges that motivate the musician's decisions to establish a career in the music field. I invite you to take a deep breath and a step back to think about what influenced you to choose a career in music (or any other career if you are not a musician or used to be an active musician). This book is not intended to be a road map or to be full of "how-to" tips. Rather, I hope each chapter will illustrate ways to think about what you have done or are doing in music and how you may feel satisfied or impeded with your aspirations.

As a musician, psychologist, and psychoanalyst, I always have felt it important to probe beneath the melody and think about more than the "obvious" notations in the score and melodies in the mind. Playing and teaching music is part of who you are as a person, not just what you "do." As a person with a talent and a long life history that accompanies you into your music profession, you have something unique to contribute to others and to yourself. I am not going to address the healing and therapy that are associated with music therapy (a field all in itself) or the newer interest in neuroimaging to discover brain (anatomic) functions of the mind (which is not anatomic), where feelings are experienced. The pandemic has interrupted your trajectory and your wishes. The future remains uncertain. Your goals may have already changed from what you initially intended to do in music—or may change as a result of the difficult time in history in which we find ourselves. You may find that a music career, particularly in performance, may continue not to be a full-time, well-paying job but may remain a lifelong relationship. You may find that working as a partner in a community-based endeavor is gratifying as you think outside the classical-music box. Music is a life journey—as such, there are twists and unexpected turns that may lead to both unexpected challenges and gratifications.

As a highly educated and skilled musician, you have an education and developed skills that have taught you to think creatively, to analyze deeply, to express intense emotion through sound, and to be able to communicate with others, even when you may feel unsure of yourself with performance anxiety and various self-doubts. I hope you will think about your relationship with music.

As I think about writing on the career choice of musicians, I feel both angst and hope. I believe the word choice should be plural, choices. Music careers can be an end in themselves but also a foundation for creative ideas using music that go beyond the concert hall and teaching studio. Music is versatile and has an important role in bringing peace and healing—an aural "heard" version of "herd" immunity that was supposed to bring the pandemic to its infectious end. We were led to believe immunity would develop if people wore masks and got vaccinated to halt the virus's ravages. Traditional career choices, particularly in performance and teaching, are undergoing change, perhaps radical change, while maintaining the core values and contributions of our musical ancestors. I hope I am not sounding too naive given the gravity of what confronts us.

I accidentally came upon what evolved into my life's work driven by an unquenchable need to know more about stage fright—my own and others'. When I was at Juilliard, everyone experienced it and no one talked about it. Performance anxiety was mysterious and fearsome. I had no idea that the agonies of some of my Juilliard experience would turn into what I love to do today. It has been a long journey—often without knowing what the future held but being certain the days and years ahead would hold something valuable for music and myself to stay connected and contributive.

I returned to graduate school at the University of Michigan and earned my MSW, MA, and PhD degrees in psychology and social work and subsequently trained to be a psychoanalyst at the Michigan Psychoanalytic Institute. None of this was anticipated when I pursued music.

Little did I know that my curiosity and determination for an unknown goal would lead to a career that has allowed me to blend my music and psychology/psychoanalysis backgrounds. Now with thirty-five years of clinical experience treating musicians, writing, presenting at conferences and meetings, and being fully immersed in my work as much as or more than ever, I wanted to share some discoveries from my journey.

I had just started entertaining a flickering idea of writing another book when I was contacted by Michael Tan, editor at Rowman and Littlefield, about . . . writing a book . . . on career choice in music. What felt coincidental turned into the chapters you have begun to read. Writing this book has been a deep dive into my past and some projections toward a future that is yet unclear. Perhaps it is this unknown that is both familiar and unfamiliar that challenges me. Perhaps our mutual unknown, fueled by the pandemic, also challenges you.

This book is my testament to the power of music in the lives of musicians who contribute to society. It is a challenge to musicians, who are, in the deepest sense of the word, trailblazers throughout history. It is a comment about musicians who have found new outlets for their talent and passion that creatively made the pandemic survivable for themselves and for so many others via technology that they quickly mastered. We never choose to become mired in a pandemic and politics. Musicians have used their training and discipline to become first responders by performing on Zoom, at airports, medical clinics, offices, and malls, and in garages. Anywhere music can be played, musicians have been present.

The pandemic did, however, dramatically impact the traditional and already difficult pre-pandemic music-career landscape. Some musicians, unable to pay monthly rent and living expenses, left the profession altogether. Others considered returning to school in disciplines that would offer stable income, such as law or medicine. Musicians found opportunities to use their music training and skills to work for social-justice and interpersonal projects with children, schools, the disadvantaged, families, and the elderly. Others collaborated with like-minded colleagues to develop creative online programming. Some older musicians retired earlier than they anticipated.[1] The pandemic forced unanticipated changes and new challenges for those who had been chosen by the music profession. Musicians rose to the occasion. So did music.

The psychological determinants of choosing a career, changing a career, or leaving a career are deeply meaningful. Music has profound, life-altering consequences for the musician's sense of purpose, self-esteem, and personal identity. When aspirations and accomplishments are abruptly—or even gradually—brought to a detour or a full stop, the emotional toll can result in depression and high anxiety. Musicians can experience the loss of a career as a psychic death. It is not unusual in my clinical work to help musicians mourn their losses of their dreams and years of work, which not unexpectedly evokes earlier painful losses and separations. Gradually, many find resilience and satisfying ways to find pleasure and renew aspirations.

When one's sense of self is challenged as severely as it has been for musicians during the pandemic, the psychological cost can be high for musicians when careers are impeded, redirected, or involuntarily ended. This psychological trauma will continue long after the physical problems with COVID-19 have been meaningfully understood and better managed medically and socially.

A major question that confronts musicians making career choices in the present moment is how to understand and productively cope with a new landscape that awaits them. That same question is a major challenge that has motivated me to write this book. A deeper look into oneself as well as considering creative, sometimes out-of-the-box, opportunities to find work in music are interrelated and powerful antidotes to the "new" psychological "normal" of which musicians must be an integral part.

This book has evolved into a combination of theory, anecdotes, and a retrospective for me to communicate with you, the reader. I hope you absorb what I offer as a testament to you, the musician, and to those people who love music. I invite you to join me in this unsettling time in history and to reflect and explore with me how you can use two of the most powerful instruments you possess—your mind and your music.

Note

1. Lynn Rosen, "Changing Landscapes for Orchestra Musicians," *Senza Sordino* (October 2021), https://www.icsom.org/senzasordino/2021/10/changing-landscapes -for-orchestra-musicians/.

CHAPTER TWO

~

Musicians and Money
in the Wake of the Pandemic

In 2020, newspaper headlines predicted doomsday for the performing arts.

- "As Music Venues Shutter, Former Owners Describe Devastating Toll"
- "Virus Related Venue Closures Will Affect the Music Business for Years to Come"
- "A 'Great Cultural Depression' Looms for Legions of Unemployed Performers"

This sudden unexpected turn of events when the pandemic forced a lockdown sent shivers down the spines of musicians. Without musicians having any time to digest the alarming news, contracts were canceled or optimistically postponed, performance venues closed their doors, and schools and universities canceled classes as they quickly stepped up to a steep learning curve that would enable them to work virtually with students. Performers and those who arranged performances were overwhelmed by the disappearance of almost all professional music opportunities. Work problems that preexisted COVID-19's onslaught were exacerbated as new challenges and creative opportunities are yet to be fully realized in the twenty-first century. If we look at only statistical data about musicians' careers, we will not find a complete story. However, the available information is sobering and informative for both how it is gathered and reported and the message it conveys. Added to self-reporting, the economic situation facing musicians is staggering.

The topic of money is unavoidable in any discussion of career. Although professional musicians are often motivated by the intrinsic value of artistic expression, mastery, and performance, they must use their careers to pay the bills like anyone else. The ability to think and talk about money is related to a personal sense of how musicians value themselves psychologically, which becomes transferred onto powerful attitudes about money. It also is important to consider the value placed by society on the arts as represented in financial terms. Even within the music profession, some musicians find and win auditions for jobs in major symphony orchestras or academic appointments that pay considerably above the pay scale earned by so many talented others who remain unemployed or underemployed. What are the ingredients in addition to talent that lead to income and opportunity discrepancies, outside and within the music profession? What are some of the underlying psychological meanings embedded in the earning potential of musicians? Are there ways musicians can become better prepared for the challenges that remain during the pandemic or while working regularly and can become appropriately financially compensated at all times to benefit from an economically as well as psychologically rewarding career?

This chapter examines relevant economic issues and their psychological significance for musicians—specifically those who do not become household names, play in well-known ensembles or major symphony orchestras, or teach at a level for which they are educated—as well as economic challenges heightened by the COVID-19 pandemic.

Some Financial Facts: A Wake-Up Call

Economic issues for musicians are problematic at best and crippling at worst. Musicians' careers are distinguished from those of other highly skilled professionals in two major respects:

1. Significant negative income disparities compared to peers with similar levels of training
2. Training that typically begins at a very young age

Additional requirements for professional musicians include the capacity and flexibility to do these things:

1. Tolerate lengthy hours of solitary practice in order to develop and maintain a high level of skill on an instrument

2. Deal with the possibility and probability of assuming additional employment to supplement music jobs
3. Creatively and continuously pursue one's chosen career in the face of economic and psychological challenges
4. Cope with rejection and competition

It might appear to the layman that the performer's working hours, i.e., the time spent performing in public or teaching students, is not the typical nine-to-five job. This is correct. An average concert may fill one to two hours of playing time. What is not seen by the public is that musicians practice alone for hours, attend classes, receive private instruction or coaching, and engage in timely and rigorous rehearsals. Some performers travel long distances to reach their engagements. Teachers spend years in their education and some also perform. The musician's workweek definitely is *not* the typical forty-hour stereotype. It often is longer.

Furthermore, it is not uncommon for travel (transportation, hotel, food) associated with performance to be absorbed out of wages shared with agents or deducted from performers' fees. These work requirements, not obvious to audiences during concerts, if known at all, can place strain on personal stamina, mental and physical health, and family life. All these issues, in addition to the economics of earning an appropriate living (typically obtained from an extra job that is not in music), can induce or exacerbate psychological stress and physical illness, family disharmony, and, for some, burnout from music careers.

The issue of health care also becomes problematic for musicians, particularly for those who are self-employed freelancers. Can a musician afford to become ill, pay for medical expenses, buy a reliable car to take him or her to performance venues, or purchase a good instrument? Ironically, many musicians work part-time at restaurants to subsidize their music income, but the pandemic jeopardized the vitality of the restaurant industry and witnessed many restaurants going out of business.

The performing-artist landscape has been affected acutely by the pandemic. But that landscape had been changing dramatically since 2017 with an upward trend, as shown in various data collected by arts institutions and organizations, although it was not commensurate with other occupations. Note that the music performer is listed in a wide variety of "artist" categories that include actors, producers and directors, dancers and choreographers, musicians, and other entertainers. We lack research specific to performing and teaching musicians, but the conclusions drawn from these data are in sync with subjective reports from musicians.[1] I will be referring to music performers as "professional performing artists." At times I also will use "musician" as it refers to the music profession or music teachers. I invite you to interject your own experiences if they apply to you as you read through the data, stories, and examples that follow.

Data collected and synthesized by the National Endowment for the Arts over many years has reported that earnings of musicians are significantly below those of other highly skilled professionals as well as many unskilled workers.[2] These national data sets present economic information that add to understanding the gross disparities between and among performing musicians and other arts and non-arts individuals and groups. The National Endowment for the Arts Office of Research illustrates information on employment and unemployment for musicians in 2019 (immediately before the pandemic) and again in 2020 (during the height of COVID-19). Typical *weekly* earnings for musicians are supplied in Table 2.1 for both years.

Consider also the following information compiled by the National Endowment for the Arts between 2006 and 2020.[3] This information can help musicians gain some perspective about their economic plunge during COVID-19. Knowledge about salaries and funding puts artists in an advantageous position to negotiate fees. It is important to have a general sense of financial trends in one's occupation. My nonmusician patients are very aware

Table 2.1. NEA Data on Employment among Musicians

	2019	2020
Employed	202,000	168,000
Unemployed	7,000	42,000
Unemployment rate	3.3%	20%
Weekly median earnings	$522	$300
Weekly mean earnings	$875	$637

The NEA research analyst who provided these data noted some distortion in comparing earnings for 2019 and 2020 (which were extracted from the 2020 US Population Survey). The 2020 Survey began to break out music directors and composers from musicians and singers. The decline in earnings between 2019 and 2020 reflects not only the pandemic but also that the 2020 estimate includes earnings for only musicians and singers, who tend to earn less than music directors and composers. For comparison, in 2020 weekly median earnings for musicians and singers was $300. For music directors and composers, it was $804. Note also that there are twice as many musicians and singers than music directors and composers—118 versus 50 in 2020—which helps explain possible confusion interpreting the actual numbers reported. My appreciation is expressed for these data to Bonnie Nichols, operations research analyst, and Sunil Iyengar, director of research and analysis at the National Endowment for the Arts.

of salaries when they are in the job market and talk about appropriate salaries when they are hired. Often, musicians are glad to be invited to perform and often do not transact fees. Having managers or agents, an additional expense for musicians, would help.

Data show that from 2017 to 2019, arts employment was trending *up* but took a steep nosedive in 2020. In the third quarter of 2020, there was a decline in artist employment in that 27 percent of musicians were unemployed compared to 1.1 percent in 2019. In the creative occupations, evaluated by the Brookings Institution, it was found that between April and July 2020, cumulative losses of 2.3 million jobs were located in creative occupations. Nowhere has the effect been more immediate than in the performing arts. Compared to 2019, the gross revenue in 2020 for the top one hundred live music tours in North America saw a drop of 78 percent due to canceled events. If there is an extended isolation period by audience members during the post-pandemic time, the effect on the performing arts may be colossal. Creative solutions by arts organizations, governments, the private sector, foundations, and the public are all necessary for a revival and survival of the arts.[4]

It has been repeatedly documented by the US census and National Endowment for the Arts studies (prior to the pandemic) that musicians earn far less income over the course of their careers than other highly trained professionals. In fact, many musicians earn less than some unskilled workers. What do these findings suggest to the musician psychologically and to society more globally? What is the value placed upon the arts in general and music in particular?

What Do Musicians Contribute?

As a psychoanalyst and a musician, I find empirical data gathered by researchers painfully at odds with what musicians actually "do" in the face of economic hardship in general and particularly during COVID-19, and how they are "rewarded" or paid appropriately. Many musicians have contributed gratis, sometimes requesting donations, when offering creative programs via the internet to a distraught public longing to escape emotional disequilibrium locked down at home or venturing out to first-responder and other jobs, risking their health and their lives.

The pre-pandemic creativity and economic difficulties that have long been associated with the musician in establishing a career have been tapped by resilient musicians to establish new ways to enhance or alter their career choice during some of the darkest cultural and social moments in memory.

It is important to emphasize this aspect of musicians' need to create and not merely focus on the concrete topic of money—to consider the function of musicians' emotional assets and vulnerability. I suggest that the psychological traits exhibited by musicians that attract them to their careers also enable them to cope creatively with adversity and challenge even when no or low economic rewards are offered. These attributes are most brilliantly evident in how musicians approached the pandemic and demonstrated yet again their important role in society. While noble and valuable in many respects, the musician's generosity that accompanies the need to create does not solve the economic dilemma of the low financial status of many musicians.

The Musician as "Product"

It helps to place a historical perspective around this topic to more fully appreciate current issues and future directions. For example, there have been suggestions for years about how to increase productivity and income in the performing arts. Some writers have related the performer's income with that of arts organizations' budgets. Arts organizations often do not keep pace with the general economy, implying that performers' incomes represent this discrepancy in the fees they are paid. Some people have conceptualized the musician as a "product" that is paid for by consumers.

A reportedly anonymous memorandum appeared in London in 1955 that suggested "novel" approaches to increase productivity in the performing arts when performance is considered a "product." This memorandum, cited below, was made by an engineer after this person attended a symphony concert:

> There seems to be too much repetition of some musical passages. Scores should be drastically pruned. No useful purpose is served by repeating on the horns a passage which has already been handled by the strings. It is estimated that if all redundant passages were eliminated, the whole concert time of 2 hours could be reduced to 20 minutes. . . . Not only was the pianist carrying out most of this work by 2-handed cooperation, but was also using both feet for pedal operations. Nevertheless, there were excessive reaches for some notes on the piano and it is possible the redesign of the keyboard to bring all notes within the normal working area would be of advantage to this operator. . . . In many cases the operators were using one hand for holding the instrument, whereas the use of a fixture would have rendered this idle hand available for other work.[5]

This passage demonstrates the absurdity of applying normal economic notions of efficiency and productivity to musical performance. It is impossible to measure objectively what constitutes a "live performance." What is clear is that a music performer is much more than a "product" from whom "labor" is purchased by the consumer (e.g., the audience).

The renowned economists William Baumol and William Bowen maintained that the income gap experienced by music performers (particularly those who perform traditional classical music concerts) is different from other economic enterprises.[6] This is explained, in part, by the realities of the profession rather than by the tongue-in-cheek recommendation about eliminating repetitions and using one foot for pedal operations. These two economists compare performance with other types of labor and outlay of time that involve automobile production, which has diminished production time due to advances in technology. The amount of time and effort a performer spends in practice plus giving a performance cannot be decreased significantly. Think about this when comparing music "production" to automobile production: It will always take approximately forty-five minutes to play a standard classical symphony or piano concerto, which underscores that music performances as "products" are trapped economically by the nature of their "technology." While modern technology and mass media clearly make the arts available to more people than live concerts do, the competition from the media for an audience often has affected performing organizations adversely—particularly ticket sales.

Creative Responses to the Pandemic

Musicians enjoy and love their work. They are generally unwilling to abandon the pursuit of professional opportunities to express themselves on their instruments. The psychological, i.e., internal, satisfaction obtained from being a musician has been referred to as "psychic income" by Baumol and Bowen.[7] Emotional pleasure is thought to be sustaining when real dollars are not forthcoming. This sounds like a version of the romanticized "starving artist." Emotional pleasure is neither romantic nor sustaining. Musicians who are starving for appropriate income and opportunity to play or teach can burn out or be forced to consider other professional options. Many are starving for appreciation and appropriate financial compensation. Finding this compensation may be easier said than accomplished and the difficult search has an effect on musicians' self-esteem as well as income.

Since the 2020 lockdown in the United States due to the global pandemic, many definitions of the career of the "musician" are in need of re-evaluation. Those who perform but are not guaranteed appropriate contracts (which include health and unemployment benefits) could face lengthy and personally expensive periods of unemployment between professional engagements. Those who lack regular employment could have difficulty qualifying for unemployment compensation, Social Security, or health insurance. Arts organizations that engage musicians also have been under monetary siege because it literally became life-threatening to produce live concerts in auditoriums where both audiences and performers were at high risk of contracting COVID-19. These venues were shut down tight during the height of the pandemic, and they face uncertainty about new spikes of illness in the future. Options for careers in music were at great risk as numerous musicians tried to find work wherever they could—often not in music.

Typical of their creative energy, musicians and teachers began to establish ways to reach out to audiences and students via the internet in 2020 as they brought pleasure and comfort to homebound audiences. They often performed for low fees or no fees at all. Sadly, many were forced to leave their professions or cobbled together varieties of jobs because they could not find employers to hire them, even when the employers or producers wanted to do so.

A 2021 study by Megan Robinson and Jennifer Novak-Leonard explores how artists' entrepreneurial work impacts their creativity and their "perceptions of community."[8] Findings indicate that a quarter of the artists maintained "engaging with community as a natural element of their practice." Others complained about funding and other structures that "burdened" their creativity. These researchers importantly recognize that "the failure of communities, and specifically funders, to recognize the primary entrepreneurial motivation of artists—a desire to maintain control of their creative process—while ignoring the considerable social good artists undertake in their practices, undermines the effort, training, skill, and labor involved in the production of art." Artists and musicians have a need to be actively involved in producing their art in creative community projects, indeed to the important need to create community itself through music and art. In other words, communities and artists can become enriched from an interactive mutual relationship between artists and funders.

Personally, I discovered offering therapy via Zoom was more effective than I expected when I had to close my private office, which precluded in-person sessions. I remember grabbing an armful of important files to bring home with me, thinking I would return in a couple weeks to resume seeing my patients in person. Both my patients and I had no idea what would happen as the days turned into months. As of this writing, the specter of COVID-19 has entered its third year. I am grateful how quickly rudimentary technological strategies allowed many people to stay connected with others. This was the case for musicians, my colleagues, and myself.

I recall a number of town-hall meetings early in the pandemic organized by the American Psychoanalytic Association (APsaA), of which I am a member. The intent was to offer support for members who found themselves, similar to musicians and teachers in private practice, scrambling, confused, and worried about their patients and to maintain connections during what became a much longer and deadlier shutdown than was ever anticipated. A regular question that was posed to APsaA members at the town halls was "What is helping you during this time?"

A regular response pointed to the emotional relief and pleasure that my nonmusical colleagues were finding by listening to music, watching creative music YouTube videos, and eventually connecting via the internet to the more sophisticated programs mounted by clever and tech-savvy musicians. To conclude one town hall, the president of APsaA played a performance of folk music—performed live on Zoom. This music elicited comments about relief, beauty, and hope in a time of mounting deaths, illness, and confusion. Masks had not yet been recommended, and people were struggling to find physical and emotional life jackets. While I do not have scientific data to substantiate what I am sharing with you, I felt within myself and heard among my colleagues a sense of hope and reassurance that listening to music brought out feelings that were unarticulated and too painful to express verbally. A soaring sense of anxiety was palpable as people were reassembling some predictable routines in their lives. How can musicians become part of the long-term healing for themselves and for others as we now have experienced the devastation enforced on us by the pandemic?

An Uncertain Future

It is too soon to predict the outcome about careers in the performing arts after our long winters of desolation and isolation. The optimistic 2017 data raises worries in 2022 and beyond. Data from the Bureau of Economic Analysis showed that spending on performing-arts tickets from July through September 2020 was $10.1 billion—roughly a quarter of the amount spent on tickets over the same period in 2019. This led some data analysts to declare, "61% of businesses in the Arts, Entertainment, and Recreation sector reported that Covid 19 continues to have large negative effects as of the last week in November 2020,"[9] and "the ongoing effects on . . . artists are some of the most visible" (and vulnerable) "of the pandemic crisis."[10]

Guibert and Hyde conclude soberly, "Solutions to sustain the arts and cultural sector—and ultimately to help shape what it looks like post-pandemic—will continue to depend on creative solutions that leverage all that arts organizations, government, the private sector, donations, and the public can bring together during a time of urgent need."[11]

How much shakiness remains lurking in the pandemic's "virtual success"? Various government relief programs have recognized the arts' dilemma and offered some assistance.[12] State arts agencies and organizations have played a role in rescue funding for the arts. More is needed. There are challenges to digital programming for both musicians and audiences. This includes the uncertainty that audiences and artists will want to shift to the technical requirements for virtual programming, and for artists the uncertainty of finding ways to pay for training and software. Will donors who helped sustain the live performing arts become less generous toward the arts if people cannot attend live events? Will technology and live-performance administrators find creative ways to collaborate so that the whole concert becomes more than the sum of its live and technical parts? Will the pandemic sensitize both the public and musicians about musicians' value (both economic and psychological) in society? The creativity that is pervasive in the arts was captured through the lens of Zoom. The economics of the performing musician will be reevaluated by administrators, public and private grantors, artists, and the public. It is time now for musicians to find and use their voices in this discussion.

It is not unusual for both musicians and nonmusicians to pursue work that has the potential to satisfy needs for approval, a sense of achievement, competency, mastery, and appropriate financial compensation. It *is* unique to performing musicians that they are not rewarded financially even as their work contributes to the gross domestic product (GDP), i.e., the overall economy of the nation. For example, in pre-pandemic 2017, "8,836 performing arts companies contributed approximately $14 billion in value and employed 122,000 people, while 22,118 motion picture and video businesses contributed approximately $74 billion in value added and employed 410,000 people."[13]

These data, not atypical in 2017, are nevertheless glaringly lower for the music profession when compared to other occupations. This realization raises questions about the psychological value and definition of the performing arts in the United States as well as the psychological motivations of the artists who are willing to perform (and donate significantly their talent and time) for fees that are not sustaining their needs while contributing to the GDP.

Sunil Iyengar, director of research and analysis at the National Endowment for the Arts, raises crucial questions: "In the darkest days of the pandemic, one often heard arts administrators pray not only that the sector would recover, but that it might experience a new birth. Yet without accounting for the distinctive characteristics and contributions of artists as workers, it's hard to imagine a policy solution that will succeed in the dual task of rebuilding the reactive economy and providing more equitable opportunities for those participating in it."[14] In other words, how do we define performing artists and how do we pay them appropriately?

Why Should You Care about Music?

I am reminded about one of my oral examinations prior to completing my PhD. My dissertation was titled "An Examination of the Commitment to Careers in Music: Alienation from Vocational Choice" (1987)—a topic that has continued to captivate my interest and provided a renewed impetus for revisiting the topic in this book under the anguish of the pandemic. I will never forget how I was enthusiastically expounding about the value of music in mental life and society. I could not comprehend how anyone could question my research or think differently from how I did. My advisor and the cochair of my committee, Jesse Gordon, posed a question that challenged me to revisit my assumption when he asked, "Why *should* anyone care about music and the arts?" I was flummoxed. Wasn't the answer obvious?

I have never forgotten Dr. Gordon's question as it pertained to my research and my zealous but naive assumptions. Ever since, I have heard his words in my mind as I write, give presentations, and work clinically. This book is a testament to his inquiring mind to not accept the obvious, quick answer, and to think about multiple functions and alternative explanations for complex issues. I have cited data and statistics in this chapter, perhaps more than you wanted to read. But statistical data do not and cannot completely provide answers to complex issues about the importance of the arts to musicians and their audiences.

Discrepancies between the *psychological* and the *economic* value of music and artists themselves persist as a leitmotif when thinking about work for musicians in 2022 and beyond as they did in 1987 when I posed similar, and as yet unanswered, questions. I have had many years to further my postdoctoral education to revisit earlier assumptions as I also worked clinically with numerous musicians and other performers. I have heard about career choice, performance anxiety, family values, economic hardships, and work challenges. I have tried to help talented people disentangle internal conflicts and interpersonal relationships. I have seen people continue on their chosen path while some made detours and others took new roads. I have tried to help people find their voices to make informed choices. I have tried to be a sensitive listener who helps people feel understood.

Iyengar asks, "Where do teaching artists fit into the equation? . . . We refer to arts' value of public health strategies. How do artists find themselves partnering effectively with organizations, in clinical and non-clinical settings, to build trust in community health providers? . . . We talk about the economic impacts of the arts—but how do we measure the opportunity . . . that lack adequate support systems for artists?"[15] I suggest that performing artists *are* teaching artists who have inherent value and who bring value to society in communities through conventional programming and nonconventional offerings, including novel venues.

Addressing his own question, Iyengar maintains, "Statistics carry more than academic value. They can be viewed as cautionary notes for arts funders and policy-makers . . . that seek to recruit artists for cross-sectional purposes. By attending more closely to disparities in income and opportunity across artist occupation types and across demographic subgroups, cultural planners can be more sensitive to remunerative needs of artists they seek to engage in projects outside the arts sector. . . . It's hard to imagine a policy solution that will succeed in the dual task of rebuilding the creative economy and providing more equitable opportunities for those [people's] participation in it."[16]

Musicians have many skills that are transferable in a complicated job market. What is not discussed is the emotional trauma and impact of changing career directions, much less abandoning career aspirations altogether for those people who have trained and prepared to be musicians. The recognition of powerful feelings that accompany the redirection or loss of one's lifelong dream and training has early emotional roots and lifelong consequences. Despite the multiple, sometimes "embarrassing," connotations and self-esteem issues connected with speaking about earning an adequate income, money is a topic that must become part of the musician's repertoire.

Mental health is a priority for all people, and especially for musicians who face far more than stage fright, which is a challenge and a significant deterrent for some people to persist in a professional minefield. Music educators in collaboration with professionals in the fields of mental and physical health, economics, and politics would provide a tremendous benefit to their students through addressing these issues in the classroom *and* simultaneously educating the public about the relationship between financial and mental health of performing artists just as artists reciprocally add to the mental health of our world.

Musicians and artists are not commodities or products. Importantly, economic data and the data's latent but important psychological message suggest that musicians must be incorporated into program planning and salary negotiations to be fully integrated and welcomed as cultural teachers and artistic ambassadors. Skills in salary negotiation and enhancing mental health must become routine in arts education, public awareness, and arts administration. We must acknowledge that economic considerations are integral to artists' and audiences' decisions about performing and appreciating music, even if there is no "tonic" to resolve the ambivalence this fact may bring up for us.

Your Money or Your Life

In an old comedy skit by comedian Jack Benny, who also was an accomplished violinist, Benny's character is accosted by a robber. Benny (whose comedic stage presence was characterized as a notoriously stingy man) is walking jauntily down the street. In a reverie, he seems to be unaware of anyone around him when a robber approaches him. The robber demands, "Your money or your life!" Benny pauses and does not respond. Becoming impatient, the robber repeats his demand: "Your money or your life!" The robber becomes more impatient: "Hey, bud—YOUR MONEY OR YOUR LIFE!" With characteristic lack of concern or urgency, Benny replies to the insistent robber, "I'm thinking it over."

Musicians should not be forced to decide between their money or their life—that is, their music. Trying to keep your money and your life may mean stepping into uncertain waters, but it also is a path that allows for creativity and satisfying relationships within communities. As we delve further into the economics of the musician, the topic of money will be explored from a psychological perspective to expand upon concrete financial data. Just as performing is more than a "product," so too—as we will see in the next two chapters—money represents more than dollars and cents.

Notes

1. The research data is both clarifying and confusing. When identifying a musician or "artist" more generically, a variety of classifications are used by the Census Bureau of the US Department of Commerce. These broad groupings include actors, architects, dancers, designers, musicians and composers, painters and sculptors, photographers, radio and TV announcers, and entertainers not classified elsewhere. The term *performing* artist encompasses actors, dancers, musicians and composers, and radio and TV announcers. The artist and performing-artist groups also include people at least sixteen years old in the US labor force who are employed, self-employed, or unemployed and seeking work. However, the 2020 US census rearranged categories, compounding an already difficult data set and analysis about earnings.

Other organizations select different criteria for analysis from the US census, further confounding analysis regarding the definition of the musician. I have used the most reliable information available and necessarily made some choices to inform my comments about musician employment, given these different criteria in the literature. Arts organizations other than the National Endowment for the Arts also compile economic data on musicians and artists. These include the American Federation of Television and Radio Artists (AFTRA), the American Guild of Musical Artists (AGMA), and the American Federation of Musicians (AFM). Many performers hold memberships in multiple organizations and some hold no memberships. Some musicians are self-employed.

2. Sunil Iyengar, "But What About the Artists?," National Endowment for the Arts, September 2, 2021, https://www.arts.gov/stories/blog/2021/what-about-artists.

3. "Artists and Other Cultural Workers: A Statistical Portrait," National Endowment for the Arts, April 2019. https://www.arts.gov/sites/default/files/Artists_and _Other_Cultural_Workers.pdf. While categories under the umbrella label of "artists" include those of nonmusicians, there is a general trend that includes musicians that becomes clear as we look at some relevant figures. Data collection for artists is complex due to the broad range of jobs that are statistically categorized as the "arts" or culture.

4. G. Guibert and I. Hyde, "ANALYSIS: COVID-19's Impacts on Arts and Culture," week of January 4, 2021. https://www.arts.gov/sites/default/files/COVID -Outlook-Week-of-1.4.2021-revised.pdf.

5. Anonymous, *The Bulletin of the American Association of University Professors* (Autumn 1955): 165–6.

6. Baumol and Bowen, *Performing Arts*.

7. Baumol and Bowen, *Performing Arts*.

8. M. Robinson and J. Novak-Leonard, "Refining Understandings of Entrepreneurial Artists: Valuing the Creative Incorporation of Business and Entrepreneurship into Artistic Practice," *Artivate: A Journal of Entrepreneurship in the Arts* 10, no. 1 (2021). DOI: https://artivate.org/index.php/artivate/article/view/135

Data are collected about musicians periodically through various census agencies. This includes the US census and organizations such as the National Endowment for the Arts, the Arts and Cultural Production Satellite Account (ACPSA), and the US Bureau of Economic Analysis. It is difficult to be precise in reporting statistics about performing artists because the field of "culture" and a "creative economy" is collapsed into various categories by those who design census and survey data. However, trends and figures are clear enough among all reputable studies to indicate year after year that many music performers (excluding superstars in popular or classical music) earn less than those professionals in other highly skilled professions. Even when working, performing artists earn far less, on average, than do many other types of artists. The lower-paying categories include "artist occupations in which non-White and Hispanic workers are more highly concentrated" (Iyengar 2021, 4).

9. The Artist Labor Force was reported in July–September 2019 and 2020 as reported in the US Census Bureau's Census Small Business Pulse Survey.

10. Guibert and Hyde, "ANALYSIS."

11. Guibert and Hyde, "ANALYSIS."

12. Loans through the Small Business Administration's Paycheck Protection Program; the Music Disaster Relief Grant in Austin, Texas; a relief fund in Massachusetts; and portions of the CARES Act, by which funds are distributed by state governors.

13. The analysis of arts data is complex and more so by the aggregation of a broad range of arts industries such as film visual darts, performers, musicians, architects, graphic designers, and curators. Additionally, the arts contribution to culture and the economy may be supported by nonprofit organizations, promoters, and other professions that are represented in the economic impact on society. However, the data do highlight the plight of the music performer sufficiently that the point is made about the inequities for this group of professionals. The data cited here are through the partnership among the ACPSA, the US Bureau of Economic Analysis, and the National Endowment for the Arts from December 14, 2020.

14. Iyengar, "But What About the Artists?" 3.

15. Iyengar, "But What About the Artists?" 2.

16. Iyengar, "But What About the Artists?" 4.

CHAPTER THREE

~

Musical Development and Psychological Development

"I cannot write in verse, for I am no poet. I cannot arrange the parts of speech with such art as to produce effects of light and shade, for I am no painter. Even by signs and gestures I cannot express my thoughts and feelings, for I am no dancer. But I can do so by means of sounds, for I am a musician."

—Wolfgang Amadeus Mozart, November 8, 1777[1]

Imagine you are at a social event and are introduced to someone you do not know. In conversation, the person asks you about yourself. Would you, like Mozart, respond, "I am a musician"? Many people identify themselves by what they "do," that is, their "work." Typically, work is intimately tied to how we feel about ourselves; for musicians, it is also tied to how we express our deepest thoughts and emotions.

Musical development, as a part of psychological development, is deeply connected to our sense of who we "are" as well as what we "do." A career in music occurs over a lifetime, often beginning unknowingly in childhood. When Mozart made his statement about being a musician, he was twenty-one years old. With the help of his father (a well-known violin teacher), he had begun piano lessons at age three; composed by age five, when he could play anything he heard by ear after hearing it once; and toured Europe when he was six. Similarly, your identity as a musician develops over your life span and is bound up deeply with who you "are" and what you "do."

As will be illustrated, various key experiences throughout life revive both earliest alliances and misalliances with parents and significant others. Musicians develop relationships with teachers, with their employers, with their instruments, and with their audiences who respond through applause (a nonverbal but also pleasurable sound that signifies approval and enjoyment).

Because of the psychological potency of music, a career in music can be both highly rewarding and devilishly problematic. We may think of work as a way to pay the bills, but we also use it to meet needs that we are only dimly aware of. In psychodynamic jargon, basic needs for love and security for any individual tend to become sublimated—or redirected—into work. For the musician, the realization that earliest caretakers are literally life-giving and nurturing becomes projected later onto teachers and audiences. It is not a difficult leap to appreciate how roadblocks such as performance anxiety can be inhibiting and debilitating for those musicians who consciously or unconsciously fear rejection or disapproval from audiences or parents.

A discussion of developmental issues will help clarify the contrapuntal and complex features of personality embedded in human development that lead to a career choice in music. All the experiences that predate commitment to a career have bearing on occupational choice—for musicians and nonmusicians alike.

Erik Erikson: Development Over a Lifetime

The psychoanalyst and educator Erik Erikson (1902–1994) created a model that integrates emotional, physical, and social development over one's entire lifetime. Erikson's work is detailed in his classic book *Childhood and Society*.[2] His theory that pertains to human biopsychosocial development is as relevant today as it was when his book was first published in 1950. This model is relevant for understanding career choice among other features of human life. Here I consider Erikson's model of development as it pertains to music and music careers in particular.

Erikson's work extends a classical theory of mind, which typically asserts that once children reach a certain age, generally late adolescence and young adulthood, they solidify their identity, particularly around career. Erikson maintains that people grow emotionally continuously *from birth until death*. Childhood and all relationships with parents and others (including audiences) are integrated into people's lifelong development.

Erikson's biopsychosocial approach to development illustrates that we do not totally "complete" one chronological stage of our lives, shed its challenges, and move on, unencumbered by prior emotional conflicts—as is the implication in Abraham Maslow's hierarchy of basic needs.[3] In Erikson's schema, we do not (cannot) totally resolve all age-appropriate issues before we move to the next chronological stage of our lives. Our birthdays do not stop coming, but our emotional development may be hindered or even slip backward during times of stress only to reappear as challenges at later ages. I witness this occurring in the problems that people present in therapy in which old issues resurface and personal history repeats in new variations. They (and I) find it challenging and satisfying to resolve some unfinished business so that they can continue to evolve less encumbered by old ghosts that have remained in the mental nursery.

A cellist, Bill, explained his attraction to music as a child: "The cello was something special that I did . . . and when I was in school I did it better than anybody else. My parents were proud of me, and other people applauded me when I played in school." Bill attended music camps during the summers and reported that "I met people that were very similar to myself . . . and I really liked that. And that gave me confidence. I met people out there who spoke the same language and so, when I'd go back to school, I'd feel a lot more confident because I knew that I had a niche in life with my music." Over many years of working with musicians, I have learned from Bill and from many others how playing music as a child and later as an adult provided a sense of uniqueness, comfort, and self-expression. Music sustained them when pressures in day-to-day environments and past and present relationships presented obstacles.

Psychological (and musical) growth does not occur linearly like a jet airplane taking off from the runway and rising straight upward into the clouds. People, and their careers, encounter turbulence and stormy weather conditions that require detours and sometimes discomfort. Skill, flexibility, training, ability to problem-solve, and greater understanding of oneself allow the pilots (or the performing musicians or educators) to have the confidence and ability to alter their courses so that all is not lost (and performers and performances do not crash). With professional help and new insights, smoother flights and safe career landings can feel less jarring or career ending.

"Ratios": Life as a Balancing Act

Erikson speaks of "ratios" when describing the resolutions of opposing feelings, thoughts, and behaviors through every stage of life. Each stage is cumulatively influenced by previous stages. This perspective suggests that we never fully resolve what ego psychologists call "conflicts" but rather discover our best adaptations (or "favorable ratios," i.e., a good-enough balance) to cope more

Table 3.1. Erikson's Eight Stages of Development

Stage	Age	Crisis	Favorable Outcome	Tasks
1	Birth–1	Trust vs. mistrust	Hope	Feeding, nurturing
2	2–3	Autonomy vs. shame and doubt	Will	Potty training, walking, talking
3	4–6	Initiative vs. guilt	Purpose	Exploration
4	7–12	Industry vs. inferiority	Competence	School, skill development
5	13–19	Identity vs. role confusion	Sense of self	Social relationships
6	20–34	Intimacy vs. isolation	Love	Love relationships
7	35–65	Generativity vs. stagnation	Parenthood	Accomplishments, nurturance
8	65+	Ego integrity vs. despair	Wisdom	Reflection, fulfillment

Adapted from Erik Erikson's "Eight Ages of Man" epigenetic chart in *Childhood and Society* (New York: W. W. Norton & Company, 1950), 273.

effectively with the competing wishes and fears that we all experience in our mental lives. One's sense of personal and professional identity in any career evolves from a series of both resolved and unresolved emotional milestones throughout life. Erikson's ratios refer to a "favorable" or "unfavorable" balance achieved, sometimes with the assistance of professional help. Favorable, adaptive "ratios" become embedded in flexible biopsychosocial timetables rather than exact ages, as the following chart indicates.

Taking a wide-angle and lifelong view of our personality and emotional development, with a focus on eight individual stages, is meaningful as we begin a deeper exploration of career decisions. For example, a performer learned that it was not *only* the cold temperature of the room that made her unable to play an instrument with a secure technique. She complained about her symptom of cold hands and other conscious realistic reasons to explain why she felt uncomfortable. However, I also learned that the performer had a very "cold" and distant mother—now represented by her fears about audience reception or rejection—whom she felt she needed to impress in order to feel loved. Psychological pressures experienced by the performer to impress the "cold," rejecting audience or parent were "explained" by the coldness of the room temperature that prevented a dazzling technique required by the performer's harsh ego and superego, which magically would result in a warmer attitude from her "cold," distant parent.

Fantasies and beliefs carried over from earlier childhood, including magic thinking about "making" things happen and "making" people like you, become modified through deeper psychological understanding. Revised and reexamined, old thoughts can revise symptoms, projections, and need for external explanations (e.g., the cold room) from earlier developmental stages when thinking was very concrete. Bringing new understanding to old problems is eye opening, comforting, and healing.

When a more favorable ratio is achieved between the major opposing dispositions at a given stage, psychological growth continues to a more mature and satisfactory way of reducing internal pressures. Under duress, individuals typically retreat emotionally and regress to earlier stages of development without realizing there is unfinished emotional business. Some unfinished psychological homework is lurking in their emotional undergrounds.

No performance is "perfect." No individual is flawless. Optimally, music performers can find flexible-enough strategies to rethink and rework ineffective earlier psychological "solutions" (that may have been effective at one time) when they remain open to new options to free themselves from the lurking ghosts haunting mental life. These mental apparitions appear unexpected and unwanted. We develop resilience by recognizing and making peace with our uninvited intruders.

Identity as a musician is connected to how we cope with, not avoid, our lifelong enduring psychological, biological, and social development at every life stage. We can learn from regressions about disappointments as well as from forward movement and find success that we never realized was possible. Deep, substantial, satisfying change is more complex than simply thinking positively, avoiding looking inward, or working harder, but it can be attained through revisiting and revising persistent ineffective coping strategies.

I am reminded of a cartoon I saw years ago. It showed a man on a bicycle, huffing and puffing as he rode with a monkey on his back. It was unclear where he was going. I fantasized that his destination was his therapy appointment. The bicyclist looked worried and distracted. Next, we saw the man riding his bicycle back in the opposite direction. This time, the monkey was sitting next to him in a sidecar. The man looked relieved and was pedaling less furiously. He no longer was carrying his metaphorical heavy emotional weight behind him. The monkey was more observable to him and was no longer a heavy burden or out of sight. In fact, the monkey was now in the sidecar, suggesting the heavy (psychological) burden on the man's back—or in his mind—had been removed or at least was better balanced. There was a lighter emotional weight upon his shoulders.

As you might surmise, this was an outcome of reaching a favorable "ratio" of a preexisting impediment experienced by the bicyclist. The problems we carry around unacknowledged and undiscussed can feel like heavy weights on our backs (and inside our minds). They can be dislodged and revised adaptively. While still present (in a sidecar seat), heavy and haunting issues can become less formidable when viewed from a different perspective when they no longer weigh us down emotionally or take a toll physically.

Carolyn's Monkey

Carolyn was devastated when confronted with an injury that required surgery and threatened her capacity to play her instrument. She feared that if she couldn't play her instrument as well, her music career would end. She worried if she would still be "anybody" if she could no longer play her cello. She eventually realized that she was the same person whether she performed or not, but the emotional challenge and cost to her sense of self was troubling her significantly when she called to make an appointment. We worked for a long time on understanding what the loss of career goals meant to her sense of herself as a competent and uninjured individual. She came to realize that she had experienced the threat to her professional identity as a musician, which she experienced as a deep, devastating psychological and bodily assault. Her agonized feelings conveyed that her career and self-esteem were intertwined in a life-or-death issue that depended on how well she performed.

Tied to this fear were earlier losses and several childhood surgeries when she recalled being put to sleep or being rolled away on a stretcher from her mother when taken to the operating room. Her adult fears about injury and surgery to fix her "broken body" (her words) and to be out of control (asleep) and taken from her mother were revived and related to her adult fears of her injury and surgery that may take her away from her beloved instrument and the adoring audience. In our therapeutic relationship, she began to worry I would leave her if she did not say the right words that would please me. Her catharsis was palpable when she was able to understand how she psychologically transferred "then" (early childhood trauma) to "now" (as a young adult making a career choice). As we worked through her early trauma in our explorations of how her past was reappearing in her present, Carolyn was able to put her "monkey" into a different perspective in a sidecar. She transformed her fear of bodily and psychological injury into a more favorable "ratio" which permitted her not to catastrophize despite reassurances from her doctor.

It became clear to me, and in time to Carolyn, how profoundly her identity was allied with her early life experiences of trauma and adult professional sense of self-worth related to her body, upon which she relied to play her cello. Not insignificant was her memory of being taken away from her mother and put to sleep (her metaphor for musical death)—a fear that persisted and reappeared when faced with surgery years later in her life. Over time, we were able to connect her fears to frightening early trauma, which brought an adaptive resolution to the worry of "not being *anybody*" (her words) if she could not perform when she feared damage to her body. She began to realize that she was *somebody* even if not actively performing.

Reverberations of her sense of her body's integrity and its loss was a consistent theme in our work in which her body, mind, and livelihood were connected and threatened. Her earlier trauma became better understood and psychologically adaptive in the context of her present life. Carolyn now could reframe her fears with understanding and could trust that others would and could help her. Her surgery was successful, and she resumed her career feeling less psychological pressure.

While having a career in music can be intrinsically rewarding, it also is possible that such a career, so intimately connected with one's sense of body and mind, can pose psychological threats, along with financial challenges, when a musician encounters personal, bodily, economic, social, or musical obstacles. Now, as COVID-19 has led to canceled performances, darkened stages, and indefinite isolated confinement—and we are simultaneously experiencing oppression and racism, climate change, gun violence, economic and social uncertainties, and political upheaval at home—many musicians are facing intensified challenges as they manage their multiple needs to nourish their self-esteem, reach out to others, and find meaningful work.

Erikson's Eight Stages for the Musician

I will summarize and briefly illustrate the Eight Stages of Man in the sections that follow and hope that you treat yourself to reading Erikson's entire book and thoughtfully applying his ideas to yourself.[4] You will recognize some of your habits, feelings, and thought patterns about events going on both around you and inside your mind. Hopefully you will revisit some of your personal history and recall some of your memories, experiences, feelings, and relationships. What stage do you think you are in now? Do you recognize how some of Erikson's stages resonate in your experiences and in your career choice?

It is worth particularly emphasizing that there is no "good" or "bad," "right" or "wrong" connotation to this discussion. Think about yourself and your decisions as they relate to your personal development, your genetic givens, and your social surroundings since all three areas pertain to who you *are* (a person) and what you *do* (music). My emphasis upon lifelong development invites the opportunity to reflect upon the idea that there is always more that can be experienced and understood in order to build upon that which has been accomplished (or not) in earlier stages. Each of us is born a "whole" person-in-progress.

In organizing Erikson's Eight Stages, I am borrowing some labels typically applied to Beethoven's compositional stages—Early, Middle, and Late—as I divide my discussion into early, middle, and late stages of the human life cycle, which are discussed with emphasis on career choice.

Early Stages (Stages 1–4)

Stage 1: Trust Versus Mistrust (Birth to Age 1)

Psychological development and personality development begin in the nursery. Music careers, for some people, also can begin (unknowingly) in the same place. The newborn's cries are music. Infants communicate from their earliest moments of life through sounds which include gurgles, coos, and other interactive aural and tactile exchanges. This communication suggests that others—parents at first, subsequently teachers, audiences, and other people—care about newborns and can be relied upon. Responsiveness from others is critical to sustaining life since newborns are totally helpless and dependent on their parents physically and emotionally to stay alive. Gradually, babies sense that their cries and gurgles elicit responses, and that they can control parents to satisfy their needs and to supply basic necessities and comforts—for example, feeding them, changing their diapers, and holding them—which emotionally indicates attentiveness, security, and love. The infant's mouth, eyes, ears, and skin literally "take in" the world through sound, eating, vision, hearing, and touch. Parents supply psychological nutrients through their care, reliability, and attention to their babies' needs. Infants develop a "feeling" that the world and people around them are reliable—or unfortunately, sometimes not.

Responses by others to the infants' cries and sounds begin to shape lifelong attitudes toward the self and others. If a baby's musical cries and sounds are neglected, the baby might become insecure and mistrustful of the ability to influence others later in life. These powerful formative interactions are not understood by infants on any conscious level, but they are instilled neverthe-less in their emerging emotional awareness through the body. The earliest exchange of responsive sounds is communicative and forms the basis for gaining attention and control from others. Such aural attunement is a primal experience of being "in tune" with another person musically. This earliest communication through a sonic and bodily relationship between children and parents is a precursor for later interactions with others. While these earliest interactions do not predict career choice, they do prefigure it if making sound eventually is expressed through music.

The satisfaction of basic needs and psychological nourishment from significant others provides the earliest foundation for lifelong emotional growth. Over time, children gradually find the capacity to love and reassure themselves and to trust others. Infant-parent "paradise" is lost for the first time (in a healthy way) when babies are sensitively weaned and learn that every cry does not elicit an immediate response. The babies have to wait (however brief, the delay is experienced by infants as interminable) for the gratifications of food, being held, and other comforts, which requires them to begin to develop tolerance for delay and frustration. Self-soothing during the short absence of parents or at bedtime or other times of separation ideally becomes an important learning and coping strategy for lifelong emotional growth.

Babies' thumbs, favorite toys, garments, or blankies may acquire special meaning to children to help tolerate parental separations (transitions) while symbolically keeping the parents close. These special objects or sounds comfort young children as they near the end of their first year when mother is unavailable, even briefly, to satisfy every gurgle and cry immediately—unlike urgent signals in infancy when basic needs for survival ideally were satisfied as immediately as possible. Those special "objects" of significance can continue into older childhood and adulthood. While some adults continue to love toy stuffed animals, they develop other meaningful reminders to feel emotionally safe and loved, sometimes wearing special jewelry or clothes or carrying beloved photographs with them. The list is as long and creative as there are people who internalize beloved others through mental representations of them. We mentally hold onto our "transitional objects," a term introduced by child psychologist D. W. Winnicott. These objects are internalized also as thoughts or comforting images in our minds. Music also serves this same purpose aurally of a connection to loved ones who are out of sight and earshot but not out of mind.

A five-year-old child announces her decision to her mother about something very special she wants to take with her as the family is packing to leave home for a vacation. She announces, "I am going to bring the socks that Gramma gave me on our trip." The child becomes quiet and then announces confidently (using a new word she has just discovered), "*Actually*, I don't need to wear Gramma's socks to think about her because Gramma is in my heart!"

This substitution of a mental memory of Gramma by taking the concrete gift of the socks and then the mental image of Gramma sweetly illustrates how children—and adults—can keep loved ones close when those loved ones are not present in person.

Importantly, the child dearly values "something . . . perhaps . . . a word or tune" in addition to the traditional teddy bear or beloved blankie, which becomes vitally important to infants at the time of going to sleep. These beloved chosen objects are a defense to ward off the anxiety of separation from mother or father. Winnicott emphasizes, "This object or a mental substitute continues being important. The parents get to know its value and carry it around when traveling. The mother lets it get dirty and even smelly, knowing that by washing it she introduces a break in continuity in the infant's experience . . . that may destroy the value of the object to the infant. . . . The pattern of transitional phenomena begins to show at about 4-6-8-12 months. Purposely I leave room for wide variations [for the age at which this phenomenon develops]."[5]

In what Winnicott calls "good enough situations," there is a mutual attunement between parents and children.[6] This creates a healthy balance ("favorable ratio") between trust and mistrust in children's internal and external world. People care. They are reliable. They do not abandon you. If people leave, they return. Babies begin to develop a capacity to feel secure.

These earliest experiences of newborns can provide a foundation for those who, many years later, choose music (and other occupations) as their career. From lullabies to music boxes to parents' voices to instruments, musically talented individuals can begin to develop confidence and appreciation from others on as-yet-unknown journeys toward music later in life, either as professionals or as music-loving amateurs.

Stage 2: Autonomy Versus Shame and Doubt (Ages 2–3)

Babies become toddlers with all the rights and privileges of two-year-olds. To stand up vertically, to walk and no longer crawl horizontally on the floor, allows toddlers to experience the world from an entirely new psychological, physical, visual, and social perspective. Toddlers who walk and talk can begin to let go of some of the necessary dependency inherent in infancy. These are the years, typically and unfortunately labeled the "terrible twos," when toddlers realize that they are separate from parents and not just an extension of them. Of course toddlers cannot articulate this but demonstrate feelings through actions and self-assertion which include self-feeding, walking, using words, and having increased tolerance in general for parents who are out of sight. "Peek-a-boo" games, acquiring vocabulary, and potty training are developmental tasks that hold meaning for increased separation from parents and introduce a growing sense of autonomy. At first, independence is sought without straying too far from Mommy (who today we may recognize as a primary caregiver of any gender). The toddler always returns to the security of being together with her.

Violist Ernst Wallfisch, whose father was an amateur violinist, remembered the influence of music in his life before he was six years old:

> I can recall much. . . . I remember as a very small boy . . . people in our home talking, laughing, smoking cigars and making music. . . . At first all I recognized were the different sounds and many moods of what they played. . . . As I grew older . . . I can remember being lulled to sleep by all these sounds. . . . To this day, wherever I hear certain works played by a quartet it brings back a flood of memories. . . . Yes, I was thoroughly imbued with the spirit of music from the cradle.[7]

Importantly, as is emphasized by Marjorie McDonald, the word "lullaby" is composed of "lull" and "bye"—a song which soothes the baby while expressing a separation, a goodbye (or goodnight). "The words tell of the absence of an important person and assure the infant of that person's return. For the preverbal child, it is the comforting tune . . . which must convey the feeling message."[8] Adults may still own their cherished blankets or stuffed animals or recall melodies in their minds.

In her moving autobiography that details racial prejudice and professional rivalries, the venerated African American mezzo-soprano turned soprano Shirley Verrett takes us through her challenging journey to superstardom. We learn of her first role models, her parents, who became her internalized support and comfort. This led her to music, her transitional object in her illustrious career. She begins her book:

> The first sound I remember is the sound of my mother singing. Hers was a rich, full lyric soprano voice that seemed to soar when she sang certain notes, but could be soothingly mellow in the lower register. I suppose at some point I started to imitate her because the quality of my adult voice bears a similarity to hers. I am sure my affinity for singing spirituals is related to these expressions of her spirit. It was the basis of a profound bond between us.[9]

She also speaks of her father as her "greatest fan." And she remembers her beloved grandmother after she died, recalling that the "sense of security I felt holding her hand still warms me. . . . Mother even told me I resembled her."[10] How poignant that she titled her autobiography *I Never Walked Alone*.

Shirley Verrett became my dear friend after she and her husband, Lou, moved to Ann Arbor. Years before, she was an idealized star when I was a student at Juilliard and she was singing in the great concert halls worldwide. Her memory has become one of my comforting transitional objects for maintaining grace under pressure and for perseverance and dignity in the face of obstacles.

A few other aspects of Stage 2 bear mentioning. Toddlers typically convey their emerging individuality with an emphatic "NO!" "No" conveys a positive message that "I am *me*! I am separate from *you*!" The acquisition of mobility, speech, curiosity, and increasing bodily control indicates a growing sense of "my self." Tugs of war around control issues can lead to struggles and tantrums indicating frustration with the children's new mobile and verbal freedom from total dependency. Gradually, children begin to discern that using the word "no" is a way to control others. (Musicians wish to control audiences and not make a "mess" onstage, which would feel "disgusting" and humiliating.) Toddlers also love to show off by moving to music and inviting others to "look at me." They and parents play "peek-a-boo" to demonstrate that people leave *and* return, typically to gales of laughter by the children. Walking children toddle away from parents, glancing back to be sure they have not disappeared. Performers' perennial fear is that audiences will walk out but not return.

The toddler years are marked also by literal, concrete thinking to explain concepts that young children cannot comprehend abstractly. For example, a young child announces that "the sun comes up in the morning so I can see to get dressed." Another child, frightened during a nighttime power failure at home, urgently pleads, "Mommy, turn on the lights!" The toddler cannot understand that Mommy is powerless to repair the electricity that has disappeared mysteriously during an approaching thunderstorm. When the electric company restores the lights, this child compliments her "all-powerful" mother by commenting, "Good job, Mommy!"

The charming magic thinking of childhood establishes blueprints for feelings throughout life about audience acceptance and rejection due to the consequences of musicians' performances.[11]

Potty training typically occurs during Stage 2 and involves both holding onto and letting go of something both special and mysterious inside one's body. To accomplish this healthy developmental challenge brings a great sense of accomplishment and pride for toddlers and later for musicians. Pressures that emerge around toilet training and handling toddlers' healthy assertion of themselves often result in willful struggles that plant roots for doubts about their bodies and minds. Establishing or losing control of musical technique and having memory slips are embedded deeply in performance-anxiety fears. Music performers dread "losing it," "dropping notes," or "making a mess" performing in public, which would feel humiliating and hearkens developmentally back to potty training. The outcomes of Stage 2 can result in a sense of autonomy but also can lead to shame, doubt, and insecurity. Feeling more comfortable with separations from parents, discovering self-soothing strategies, and becoming healthily acquainted with one's body are implicated life long in personality and careers in music. The instrument played or music itself can serve as a transitional tune for connecting with others.

An adult's career in music, particularly in performance, encompasses infant and toddler developmental challenges and adaptations. An outcome of toddlerhood can lead to performance anxiety and fears of rejection and criticism replete with the humiliating indictment "Shame on you!," or worse, "You will be abandoned!," or the worst of all, "I do not love you."

Stages 3 and 4: Initiative Versus Guilt (Ages 4–6);
Industry Versus Inferiority (Ages 7–12)

The middle years of childhood involve the psychosocial tasks of playing games with others, finding pleasure in learning, and the emergence of a conscience (superego) about right and wrong versus being as self-absorbed and self-centered. Beginning school, having curiosity about where babies come from, and starting to notice the differences in size and gender of other children and adults are developmentally appropriate. Parents and teachers become role models as well as caretakers, who serve as extensions of parents.

Many children begin instrumental lessons during these years. The inclination for competition emerges—with both peers and parents—which extends eventually to other musicians when performing at school or other competitive events. Less adaptive "ratios" find children feeling inferior, developing anxiety about pleasing others (or depending on others to provide their self-esteem since internal resources are in short supply). Some children feel guilty and not deserving to be successful because winning, in their minds, deprives others of that honor. With good-enough guidance (notice the word "perfect" is not used), the successful negotiation of Stages 3 and 4 starts to prepare young people for the rigors of a career in music should they follow that route at an older age. Playing an instrument, which may become a transitional object along with other precious possessions, may emerge in important ways.

Psychological growth from early childhood to preadolescence increasingly includes becoming tuned into what others think of you and what you feel about yourself and others. Fitting in with the "norm" of a desired social group gradually becomes ego-nourishing as a developmental task, and anxiety and self-consciousness around being different is worrisome to children of this age.

A nine-year-old girl composed the following creative story that illustrates both her wishes and her anxiety about peer acceptance. She worked on her concerns about not belonging through writing about a centipede (which, not surprisingly, represents herself).

> Once there was a centipede, and it was going to a ball on Friday and he didn't know how to dance. . . . So, he went to dancing school, but he got so confused because he didn't know which foot to move. The teacher said, "Move this foot there and that foot there." [The] centipede said, "I don't know which foot to move." No matter what the teacher tried, the centipede could not dance.
>
> The next day was Friday and [the] centipede was so nervous. Then he finally went to the ball, but he didn't feel like dancing. And then he saw other animals dancing and they weren't all dancing the same. He realized you could do any dance you wanted. So he started to do the worm! He had so much fun and he lived happily ever after. The end.[12]

Some children show significant musical progress as they move chronologically toward late childhood and adolescence. Parents typically are delighted; the children feel a sense of competence and endorsement, and take pride in their accomplishments.

A foundation is set early in life for pleasure in making music, winning prizes and applause, achieving competence, and having a sense of belonging that takes root from interactions during the earliest years. The appreciation of childhood "laws" can inform career decisions and self-image later in life. For example, a child's fascination or fear of loud thunderstorms can be heard years later in his excitement or anxieties in thunderous-sounding music. At later ages, discomforting symptoms such as physical pains, relationship issues, and work dissatisfactions accompanied by effects such as anxiety and depression typically hearken back to earlier, perhaps more stormy, psychological and social roots such as loss of a parent, moves to new locations which include changing schools and friends, illness in self or a loved one, or a divorce in the family.

An adult patient spoke of his excited anticipation when a summer storm was brewing, relating his feelings to growing up in a place where there were periodic ominous clouds and loud thunder that were both frightening and dramatic to anticipate. He spoke also of his fondness for Beethoven's Sixth Symphony. This symphony was programmatically named the *Pastorale* by the composer and dramatically musically evokes stormy intensity (meteorological and intrapsychic by a composer losing his hearing) followed by an emotional release heard in the music to connote the storm's ending and peacefulness returning.[13]

The successful (never "perfect") negotiation (Erikson's "favorable ratios") of early childhood bodes well for the joys and travails that are inherent in the (stormy) challenges that await those who make music their career, where strong feelings, rejections, and competition abound and may evoke earlier trauma.

These reactions may be related to wishes both to win in games and to win favoritism with parents—a normal process in developmental maturation. They also resonate with making music as a way to gain "love" through applause when performing for audiences coupled with the fear that audience disapproval will be disappointing or, worse, devastatingly crushing.

Some upper-elementary-age children who have been attracted to playing an instrument at young ages make significant musical progress as they move chronologically toward puberty and adolescence. By now, many are active in choir, band, or orchestra at school and some may take private music lessons. Parents typically are enchanted; the children feel a sense of competence, endorsement by others, and pride of their accomplishments. A typical progression that deepens music involvement proceeds to performing regularly in their teachers' recitals. Some students enter music competitions. Some win these competitions. Some are not chosen. Coping adaptively with anxiety, ambition, rejection, and disappointment is a developmental and lifelong psychological task.

Middle Stages (Stages 5–7)

Stage 5: Identity Versus Role Confusion (Ages 13–19)[14]

Some disharmony and dissonance may be experienced by musicians who make a career decision during adolescence. Musical talent in young children typically is nourished and valued by the parents. Yet when adolescents announce serious intentions of becoming professional musicians, it is not unusual for some parents to replace their supportive attitudes with objections.

A pianist was struggling with her conflicted decision to major in music performance in college. She wrestled emotionally with some persistent nagging feelings: "My parents were divorced and my mother kept reminding me that musicians didn't get jobs . . . always telling me to go into the sciences. It made me mad, but I also got a little scared."

A singer shared her conflicts about her career wishes for music performance when she spoke about her father, whom she called her role model who enjoyed playing the piano as an amateur, but who unexpectedly showed his ambivalence when she was accepted at a high-level music school.

> My father would sit down and play the piano. . . . He was terrific! . . . When I was accepted into the performance program, the first thing he said was (he was there when I opened my acceptance letter), "Well, what are you going to do with music?" That was the first thing he said, and the whole time he was pushing me to go to this school and then I get in and then instead of congratulations, it's, "Well I don't know if music is such a safe thing to go into, forget it. . . ."

Adolescents cope with important questions and decisions, which include "Who am I?" and "What do I think?" Further, acceptance by peers and a more sophisticated separation and individuation from parents than toddlers' first attempts are identified by the eminent psychoanalyst and educator Peter Blos, who asserted that "adolescence has been called a second edition of childhood" which permits the individual a "second step in individuation, the first one having occurred toward the end of the second year when the child experiences the fateful distinction between 'self' and 'non-self.' A similar, yet far more complex individuation experience occurs during adolescence which leads . . . to a sense of an identity."[15]

This transformation of the question "Who am I?" into an affirmative response, "Who I am," becomes manifest in career choice, which reflects repetitions, resolutions, and reevaluations of childhood experiences. Psychologically, career decisions become internalized over many years and are closely related to one's occupational identity. This optimally occurs toward the end of the teenage years as one leaves home for college or other endeavors. In some young people, this decision is made earlier in life. I was one of those people who "knew" ever since my early childhood that I wanted to be a concert pianist when I grew up. I would never have believed you if you told me then that I would be very happy altering my career direction many years later after seriously training in music.

Music students who, by adolescence, have been playing an instrument, working with a private teacher for many years, participating in music events inside and outside school, and feeling accepted by like-minded peers and music teachers have developed a deep emotional investment in learning and performing music. I believe music itself by now has become their predominant "transitional object." In all cases, all biopsychosocial experiences have accumulated and coalesced (not concluded) significantly by the middle stage of one's life cycle.

An affair with music, associated with parental love, audience applause, and physical control of a chosen instrument through bodily technical command and emotional expression, has taken root. This finds many talented musicians not only proficient but also, importantly, identifying with music as a unique way to express themselves as a life choice. Budding professional musicians also have internalized the essence of significant people in their lives (i.e., ego ideals and role models). Eventually musicians develop the determination, often a passion, to pursue a career in music irrespective of psychological or financial realities that are documented. Musicians enter music schools and conservatories to study at a very high and demanding level. Many have never considered alternatives. This was true for me, although I, like many others, had multiple reasons for my decision about which I was unaware at the time, and which I will share in a subsequent chapter.

I continue to emphasize, as a leitmotif in this book, that at this important junction in musicians' personality development, professional identity may be threatened, compromised, or delayed as dedication to music runs head on into "negative sanctions (by parents and society) . . . in the form of derision and questions concerning the practicality of their labors, as well as their 'sanity.'"[16]

The favorable "ratio" described by Erikson may be threatened, compromised, or delayed. A mixed message automatically does not discourage some individuals intent on expressing their talent professionally and may result in intensified efforts to pursue their vocational choice in music, and at times risk estrangement from parents. The gratification of one's occupational need may supersede parental opposition, possibly at the expense of engendering anxiety or guilt in the aspiring musician. However, acquiescing to parents also is stressful if musicians bow to parental wishes and abandon their own sense of autonomy. A second attempt at individuation (identity versus role confusion) potentially is colored by new conflict and perhaps a more difficult identity crisis which casts the belief of "who I am" into "what do I do now?" I have worked clinically with many conflicted young musicians around this dilemma. This is an agonizing conflict for numerous people.

For these musicians who persist at this stage, and many do, expression and gratification of their own needs supersede parental worry, warnings, and realistic obstacles, which can increase anxiety onstage and conflicts at home. Adult musicians may have to pay a high emotional price, beyond the loss of tangible economic income, if underlying issues (unfavorable "ratios" according to Erikson's model) are not recognized and sensitively addressed as they arise. It is not unusual for symptoms to appear in the guise of stage fright in which performers are fearful of "messing up" (Stage 2) in front of an audience with memory lapses or technical malfunctions on their instrument, metaphorically evoking bodily functions that were proudly controlled (or not) during toddlerhood.

Young people, beset with self-doubt and now mixed or negative messages from significant others, challenge their own fears and do not go onto the concert stage or into the job market with assuredness of finding work. Such performers are worried about depending on an audience—or parents—if career goals are either *attained* or *unattained*. Often I hear expressions from young-adult patients that echo childhood scoldings reminiscent of Stage 2, which include "I messed up," "I dropped notes," and "I felt humiliated" in reference to themselves as musicians and their malfunctioning bodies and minds, which impede, by now, their conflicted aspirations.

It is not surprising to conceptualize identity and music career development as a parallel or at least a complementary process during the early years and throughout life. Career choice in music places performers in an unenviable position if primary emphasis is focused upon pleasing the audience—or teachers—or parents. Thus the solidification of personality and career choice in music during adolescence potentially is tinged by musicians' emotional conflicts, which may include ambiguous or outright negative messages from earliest caregivers at a crucial junction later in their life cycles. This is paralleled on a societal level particularly in the United States, where public and private support of the arts often is insufficient or mercurial, sending mixed messages to many talented people seeking work. Contrapuntal themes embedded both in career choice in music and in personality development are complex and can be consonant and also jarringly dissonant.

I would be remiss to not mention another scenario about career choice. Some parents are thrilled, often envisioning their children fulfilling some of the parents' own thwarted ambitions. Either endorsement or doubt in parental attitudes has the potential to foster self-doubt in budding professionals. To seek a career in music professionally against parental blessings or to fulfill parents' wishes can ignite the fears around letting parents—or the musicians themselves—down.

This complex dynamic played out in a vocal student's performance anxiety when singing a duet with an older man who had returned to pursue a graduate degree some years after earning his undergraduate degree. The young singer performed in a recital at the end of her junior year. The concert provided her the opportunity to show her family, particularly her father, that she could be successful. At a younger age, her father had entertained the idea of majoring in music but switched his career to business out of a desire for greater financial security. She believed he understood her music aspirations (and perhaps she understood his). As part of her solo program, she sang a duet with the returning male student. The performance resulted in disaster: "I got up there and I just forced it out and all of a sudden it was like I was hyperventilating and everything went black, and I thought, 'Oh great!' . . . I did not faint and kept singing. I don't know how I did it." She was disappointed and felt her parents were too: "It was like they were more disappointed than they were worried about me. . . . My mom was cool. She's not into music at all and she thinks it's pretty silly. . . . My dad said, 'Why did you let it happen?' . . . I got very resentful and thought he supported my music interest—and why didn't they realize I'm only eighteen years old?"

This young woman's longing for parental approval and nurturance, particularly from her father, clashed with her conflict to show, indeed to prove, musical competence to her parents. The duet during which she broke down was performed with her older male colleague, by whom she felt "intimidated."

In our work together, I helped her explore her intent about pleasing her father, who probably was not too far from the age of her vocal partner and from whom she wanted to capture approval. We came to understand that her experience of feeling intimidated by her collaborator (or, in displacement, her father) precluded her thinking of him as a colleague in performance that would have allowed her to enjoy and share her performance rather than have it undermined by anxiety, anger, guilt, and self-doubt.

Outside of her awareness but lurking in the backstage of her mind, she had no choice but to collapse in this situation. A successful performance with this older male singer combined with her buried feelings about being special to her father (and disappointing him as well due to unconsciously feeling competition with her mother) were both anger- and guilt-provoking. Failing onstage was her way of punishing herself for these feelings and making her own choices instead of enjoying success onstage unencumbered by guilt. It is not surprising that she crumbled musically and emotionally when viewed by an audience that included both her parents. In fact, every member of the audience became a potential disapproving as well as longed-for parent—intensifying her distress.

Her public breakdown evoked earlier buried but unknown wishes and feelings she developed at a younger age. Little girls want to be special to their fathers. This first special love is projected later onto the audience (or other authority figures), for whom musicians displace their wish to gain love in return for excellent performances.

Early childhood experiences cast a long shadow when young people long for intimate relationships. In later developmental stages, males and females find love with people of their choice with whom they can mutually share affection and pleasure. For musicians (and for other nonmusicians), a career choice metaphorically and psychologically represents a displacement of childhood strivings for giving and receiving love through outstanding performances and through their work. The psychological impact of infancy, childhood, adolescence, and young-adulthood cannot be overemphasized and must be addressed sensitively, often through what can be understood and interpreted in psychological treatment, and importantly be appreciated both by the students and by the institutions that educate them.

Young-adult musicians, newly graduated and seeking work, face psychological dilemmas which can lead to disillusionment, anxiety, and depression and can challenge earlier motivation. This tends to occur when the "real" work world is not particularly welcoming and idealized as were the parents of childhood. Young musicians often find insufficient financial compensation, as well as intense competition and rejection among so many highly talented people vying for too few jobs. Multiple factors that appear during Stage 5 can evoke debilitating anxiety, depression, and eventually burnout if psychological help is not sought.

Stage 6: Intimacy Versus Isolation (Ages 20–34)

During the years of young-adulthood, the intensity of youthful friendships often evolves into intimate romantic relationships replete with the vulnerabilities that come from revealing oneself to another person. For music performers, this includes opening up themselves to audiences. Mutual love, vulnerability, and admiration is a marker in both personal and professional relationships.

During this stage of life, musicians make a serious commitment to music as a "life partner." Work choices become increasingly related to one's sense of self, sense of purpose, and self-esteem. Psychological development can get stuck due to unresolved problematic emotional conflicts that surge at this time and that dip back emotionally to early-childhood precedents.

If previous development, including relationships with parents, peers, and teachers, has gone well enough, many musicians are able to deal with the challenges of the intensity and uncertainties of career and personal demands. For those individuals who have not dealt with the conflicts and crises of earlier years, the challenges of young-adulthood might feel considerably overwhelming. Some musicians may decide to leave music and seek other employment since music offers many built-in external challenges that evoke painful emotional antecedents of rejection and competition. Other musicians find challenges to their vulnerability might enhance creativity and feel determination to exert immense effort to work through difficult situations and achieve an expanded sense of competence. Instead of suffering in solitude or asking friends for advice, some people seek therapy, which helps sort out nonmusical issues that are not understood and about which musicians have been unaware.

It is during this stage of life when many musicians who have persevered to high levels of expertise in their training have graduated from their formal schooling and are seeking meaningful work to establish their professional identities. Psychologically, work choices become increasingly important to one's sense of identity and self-esteem. It does not take too long for doubts to emerge when there are repeated triggers and potential roadblocks—psychological, physical, economic, and/or social—that interfere. Now with formal education completed (for the moment, perhaps), the very real mercurial and demanding nature of a career in music, particularly in performance, is met head on.

If previous development, including relationships with parents, peers, and teachers, has gone well enough (remember, there is no such thing as "perfect"), most performers are able to deal with significant challenges, including feeling overwhelmed. For those individuals who have not sufficiently resolved ("favorable ratios") major conflicts and crises of earlier stages in development, there is increased potential that the demands of young-adulthood will exert considerable pressures.

Fears about loss of the self can result in avoidant behavior and self-doubt, loneliness, isolation, depression, anxiety, and confusion about what to do next. Performers may worry that employers will not hire them just as parents did not (or were perceived to not) supply emotional nourishment about their offspring's careers in music or, conversely, depended on their children to be successful to bring stature to the families. Additionally and importantly, musicians already have become laser focused on music (which is necessary—people cannot start music training at later ages to pursue it professionally) at the expense of diversifying occupational vision and options. It is very, very difficult to alter or lose the deeply held wish to be successful in one's chosen career and particularly in the long journey that leads to being successful in music.

Those people who pursue performance find challenges to their vulnerability are worth the effort to find ways to deal with emotional blockades, perhaps engaging in good psychotherapy and supportive friendships, which includes finding mentors. At times, music actually enables individuals to cope successfully with complex personal histories and find compensatory psychological and interpersonal outlets. Creative redirection increasingly becomes an option that begins to creep unconsciously into the awareness of some musicians. For musicians of the twenty-first century, keeping their options open has become a requirement.

I think of my career in music, originally slated for performing, as taking an unexpected, arduous, and circuitous route. My redirection ostensibly occurred with determination mixed with naivete, flexibility, risk-taking, and curiosity about myself and about others who struggled with stage fright. I gradually gravitated, consciously unplanned, into the world of psychology and social work in a different academic edition of graduate school at the University of Michigan. I went from a highly competitive and intense environment at Juilliard with an enrollment of seven hundred blazing talents to a very large and competitive liberal-arts atmosphere at the University of Michigan fourteen years after earning my Bachelor of Music and Master of Science degrees in piano performance at Juilliard.

My career and I grew up together, with support from my mother and grandparents, and later from mentors and my friends when I sustained not only major losses in my family but also the loss of my dream for a music career. I had no idea the eventual interpretation of my original dream would turn out so differently. Yet the lessons and discipline I absorbed from Juilliard fortified me in many unexpected ways when I landed in required courses on graduate statistics, psychopathology, personality theory, organizational dynamics, psychotherapy, family and individual therapy, and clinical internships—not to mention writing two prelims and, thankfully, only one dissertation. I began to understand that career choice was much more nuanced than I had considered previously.

The advice of my high school choir teacher to "keep your options open" began to make sense. Originally, I thought he did not think I had what it "took" to make it in music. Now I appreciate his foresight and wisdom. He *did* believe in me. He had confidence I could develop the necessary vision to see beyond whatever I originally set out to accomplish.

Life changed dramatically for me in personal ways as well. During the momentous year I earned my master's degree from Juilliard, my mother died. I got married not long after. Grief and joy intermingled. I had no clarity about what I wanted to do going forward professionally. It was unsettling to deal with the excruciating pain of my mother's death followed by emotional numbness including the thought, "What would my life be like without my mother? Without music?"

Stage 7: Generativity Versus Stagnation (Ages 35–65)

Mature musicians in the middle stage of Erikson's schema continue to contribute to the next generation through teaching and creative activity, which may or may not include performing. In building a legacy for future generations, transmitting knowledge and sharing music through teaching, mentoring, concertizing, presenting, and writing are important links from one's past to future generations.

It is not unusual for nonprofessional instrumentalists who began lessons in childhood but who discontinued playing for many years to restart studying their original instruments or take up different ones. Some people collaborate with colleagues by playing chamber music. Many musicians may still be active in their profession.

Feeling impoverished for a lack (or perceived lack) of creative success in earlier years may result in becoming self-absorbed, isolated, or depressed. Interestingly, some musicians have spent so many years being creative and productive that they have lost the capacity to enjoy meaningful personal lives outside their profession or to relax. In spite of professional productivity, some musicians may feel despondent or lonely as they reach the chronological age that may feel like turning back is not an option, even as moving forward still presents new choices.

Late Stage (Stage 8)

Stage 8: Ego Integrity Versus Despair (Ages 65+)

The age ranges Erikson designated for his Eight Stages in 1950 are flexible. In 2022, defining old age beginning at sixty-five feels premature. With increasing advances in mental and physical health care and research, "old" age has moved its onset to ages older than sixty-five. Some people die in their twenties, forties, or fifties. For them, these ages were both "old" and final. "Old age" is an attitude rather than a "number." I suggest that musicians' creativity knows no age limits.

Some musicians work meaningfully beyond age sixty-five. The list included here contains a few classical musicians whose names you may recognize and who worked productively into their ninth and tenth decade. A few examples of the icons include pianists Vladimir Horowitz (86) and Artur Rubinstein (95), cellist Pablo Casals (96), violinist Isaac Stern (81), composer Stephen Sondheim (91), and conductors Arturo Toscanini (89), Leopold Stokowski (95), Nadia Boulanger (92), and Leonard Bernstein (who passed away too young at age 72). Pianist Ruth Slenczynska is making a recording on her ninety-seventh birthday. There are many musicians who are not famous household names but who still contribute their talent meaningfully.

Retirement is a major career transition and another meaningful creative facet of a career choice in music. A career in music evolves into a way of life that provides an important lifelong anchor for one's identity. A career in music represents much more than a job or an age.

Balancing fulfillment and satisfaction with regret is an emotional task that confronts every person who lives into older-adulthood. Momentous choices made at this stage include reflecting upon how our lives have been lived. Years of familiar routines in daily life may become new avenues for opportunity, different for each person. Musicians have a chance to consolidate past challenges of work and personal experiences that have ripened (or remain yet to be discovered and examined) over a lifetime. For those people who have navigated the challenges of careers with a sense of satisfaction, there is a feeling of pride. For those who feel they have fallen short of their goals and who feel more regret than pleasure, there typically is a nagging sense of despair and remorse. Life will not last long enough to start over.

The psychological, social, and occupational paths that intersect for musicians are never more poignant than at the beginning and end of their careers. Retirement and aging are a time of interesting transitions and reflections as well as the time for the realization of life's limitations.

During Stage 8 of the life cycle, there remain opportunities to share your musical gift with others and to value your unique legacy accrued from your life's work in music.

Notes

1. Letter from Wolfgang Amadeus Mozart to his Father. Mannheim, Nov. 8, 1777, In *The Letters of Mozart and His Family*, Trans. Emily Anderson. Vol. 1, Second Edition, Macmillan. London.1966.

2. Erik Erikson, *Childhood and Society* (New York: W. W. Norton & Company, 1950).

3. Maslow maintains that one cannot progress into a higher, more adaptive stage of emotional development until the previous stage is completed. A. H. Maslow, "A Theory of Human Motivation," *Psychological Review* 50, no. 4 (1943): 370–96.

4. Adapted from Erik Erikson's "Eight Ages of Man" epigenetic chart in *Childhood and Society*. This revised chart also is helpful in thinking about stage fright and the biopsychosocial tasks involved in understanding performance anxiety as detailed in *Managing Stage Fright* (Nagel 2017, 124).

5. D. W. Winnicott, "Transitional Objects and Transitional Phenomena," *International Journal of Psychoanalysis* 34 (1953): 89–97.

6. Notice the term "good enough," not "perfect," is used by Winnicott. People of all ages get into "psychological trouble" when they feel they and others must be "perfect."

7. Ishaq Arazi, "One Plus One Equals One," *American String Teacher* 19, no. 1 (1969): 6–10, 26.

8. M. McDonald, "Transitional Tunes and Musical Development," *The Psychoanalytic Study of the Child* (1970): 515–25, 503–20.

9. S. Verrett, *I Never Walked Alone* (Hoboken: John Wiley and Sons, Inc., 2003), 3.

10. Verrett, *Never Walked Alone*, 14.

11. The children who made "magic" statements in the above examples all became very competent nonprofessional artists or musicians.

12. Now a young adult, this girl has developed strong writing skills and also deepened her creative artistic talents as she moves toward her career goal as a photojournalist, which she is pursuing in college.

13. By the time of the Sixth Symphony's premiere in 1808, Beethoven had lost 60 percent of his hearing, was depressed, and penned his famous Heiligenstadt Testament, a letter to his brothers in which he seriously considered suicide due to his devastation in losing his hearing. At the conclusion of the letter, he decided not to harm himself and to promote peace through his work. Beethoven was fully deaf by 1816 when he was forty-six years old. It is thought that his Sixth Symphony represented sounds he could hear only inside his head during his inner turmoil and search for peace.

This is one of only two symphonies to which Beethoven gave a programmatic "name," i.e., *Pastorale Symphony* or *Reflections of Country Life*. The composer is purported to have said the symphony is "more an extension of feeling than painting." It was premiered December 22, 1808, in Vienna along with his Fifth Symphony purportedly in a four-hour concert. Each movement of the Sixth Symphony has a programmatic name. Notably, the fourth movement depicts a thunderstorm that is followed by the fifth movement, depicting sunshine after the rain. Beethoven was noted for walks in the country—and some musicologists have suggested this symphony speaks to Beethoven's despair (stormy feelings) with his deafness and he longed for the psychological peacefulness of country life and nature particularly if his deafness could not be cured. In 1807, Beethoven wrote, "Anyone who has the faintest interest in rural life will have no need of descriptive titles to enable him to imagine for himself what the composer intends" (Antony Hopkins, *The Nine Symphonies of Beethoven*, 167). The five movements are titled, by Beethoven, as such: 1. Awakening of Happy Feelings on Arriving in the Country; 2. Scene by a Brook; 3. Joyful Gathering of Country Folk; 4. Thunder Storm; 5. Shepherd's Song: Happy and Thankful Feelings After the Storm. Adopted here from "Eastman School of Music Centennial Celebration," 1921–2021. Contributors to this article on Beethoven's Sixth Symphony are indicated as JF, YLiu, MER.

14. P. Blos, *On Adolescence: A Psychoanalytic Interpretation* (New York: The Free Press, 1962).

15. Blos, *On Adolescence*, 11, 23, 12.

16. M. Griff, "Fine Arts: Recruitment and Socialization of Artists," in *International Encyclopedia of the Social Sciences*, vol. 5, ed. D. L. Sills (New York: Macmillan Press, 1968), 453.

CHAPTER FOUR

~

The Meaning of Money and "Psychic Income"

Money is a taboo topic—especially how much money a person makes for a living. For many people, it is more difficult to talk about money than it is to talk about sex. A psychological perspective on the multiple meanings of money sheds light on why this reticence occurs and is relevant to the undercompensated musician. This approach to money probes beneath concrete financial figures that appear on charts, graphs, research data, and bank statements about musicians' earnings and attempts to make sense of the psychological meaning of dollars and cents. It is not intended as an exhaustive discussion on the multiple psychological meanings of money, yet it offers additional ways to think about why it feels uncomfortable to address money as openly as you would talk about, say, what you ate for lunch.

The discussion of money feels sensitive for many people, and talking about it often is avoided by couples and families and in professional circles.[1] Money can be a very delicate and heated topic that often brings couples to marriage counselors. Psychologically, money has many symbolic and metaphoric meanings in addition to concretely representing currency for buying and selling services, goods, and products.

An individual can be wealthy and feel impoverished. A musician can feel "compensated" but not earn sufficient income for basic expenses without a second job or a partner who holds stable well-paying employment. A performer can simultaneously need and want to earn money yet be hesitant to ask for appropriate fees; thus, "feeling wanted" becomes sufficient for psychic income. Money, mind, and music are difficult to describe subjectively.

Difficult does not mean impossible. As mentioned, money is a very private topic—and conversation about it is often avoided. There can be a high cost paid psychologically for avoiding discussions about money. Talented individuals possess a gift that is nurtured by hours of hard work that they share with others. This gift should not be given away lightly or frequently. Paying bills cannot be replaced by psychological sustenance and applause.

Early Issues about Giving and Receiving

The earliest sharing that is life sustaining is represented initially by the mother who nurses her newborn, thus gratifying basic needs; feeding and love become associated over time. The psychological complexities that are involved in giving emotional, life-giving nourishment (or withholding it through inattentiveness, absence, or ignoring the baby's cries) set an emotional stage for lifelong psychological growth or feelings of impoverishment, worthiness or feeling undeserving. An alternate possible outcome of not feeling emotional nourishment could be expressed through an attitude of entitlement in which individuals feel they are owed something. All these foundations about the worth of oneself are established long before dealing concretely with money enters one's awareness, life, and career.

This is not to imply that mothers consciously withhold themselves from their babies, but infants do not have a way to understand why the breast is not offered immediately or why bodily discomforts are not tended to immediately. The concept of "wait"—even a delay that is experienced as a seemingly endless second—is foreign to newborns. However, repeated lack of good-enough attention first by mothers and by other caregivers can have early and lasting consequences since babies and developing children feel that their cries (or earliest music) do not elicit immediate gratification.

Attention and Money: Symbolic Nourishment

The audience later serves as a parental representation or metaphor for the biological "mother/parent-audience" who originally nourishes and feeds the performer/baby through appreciation, attentiveness, and applause (i.e., emotional currency). It also is mothers' comfort, support, and attentive reassurance that performers must symbolically leave backstage when they take center stage. Performing solo in particular may evoke panic when feeling abjectly alone and having to prove oneself to the audience to capture this important emotional nutrient.[2] Performers crave love (nourishment) granted by the audience/mothers/parents through approving of the performers' stellar performances. This nourishment is experienced as a kind of psychic income and, as you may recall from the earlier description of psychic income in chapter 2, is very seductive.

Symbolically, money may eventually come to represent sufficient nourishment but also deprivation of basic needs throughout life. Anxiety (often experienced as stage fright) haunts performers who fear love (or, symbolically, money) will be withheld for perceived inferior, subpar performances. The two-faced portrayal of Janus illustrates the idea that money represents complex, often opposing, feelings, including feeling both needy and greedy, worthy and unworthy (e.g., being inclined to ask or not ask for professional fees). The data on income for performers and clinical experience suggest that some musicians place a lack of psychological value on themselves and that this transfers to the difficulty to be assertive about their financial needs. A number of performers feel and often rationalize that "psychic income" is sufficient since they love what they "do." Explanations of multiple symbolic meanings of money are explored by psychoanalyst Salman Akhtar, who addresses the gratification in both giving and receiving.

> It should be emphasized that miserliness is unrelated to the actual financial state of the individual. Both the rich and the poor can be miserly, and both can be generous. Tight-fistedness is the inverse of large heartedness. It is not about lack of money. That said, the problem of miserliness appears to have two faces. Subjectively, the miser is saddled with terrible anxiety; parting with money stirs up in him the dread of becoming poor and resourceless. Saving money is equated with psychic security, and the slightest monetary bleed is felt to be life-threatening hemorrhage. The miser resorts to all sorts of conscious and unconscious measures to avoid spending. Rationalization especially comes to his or her rescue; it helps stinginess masquerade as prudence. Inner tension nonetheless persists. . . . *The miser has experienced a profound and traumatizing lack of nourishment from his early caretakers.* The miser's self is split; a cruel and withholding adult triumphantly parades outside while a deprived child weeps inside.[3] (Emphasis added)

Many musicians are far from miserly in giving their talent freely (literally) but in doing so deprive themselves. Their competence perhaps illustrates feeling deprived and undeserving while their gift of talent is perceived as generous compensation to earn emotional currency.

It also is possible that children who have been given "everything" feel guilty and tend to withhold giving to themselves through not feeling deserving of a respectable income from others. Money, in this situation, becomes the currency of shame and feeling ashamed to accept more than the honorarium offered when performing a concert or negotiating a teaching salary. It becomes a little clearer why a discussion about a topic as complex as dollars and cents can be very painful and difficult.

Ann Ruth Terkel's view also emphasizes multiple meanings embedded in money: "In our culture, money is a symbol of worth, competence, freedom, prestige, masculinity, control, and security, all of which can become areas of conflict."[4] Musicians' relationship with financial issues conveys a great deal about their feelings about themselves.

Dictated by COVID-19, there was a very long intermission from attending live events. Prior to the arrival of the omicron variant in 2021, some concert promoters tried to reopen their auditorium doors. Many found requirements for social distancing and lowering attendance capacity, as well as the reluctance or refusal of some patrons to wear masks or get vaccinated, made it necessary to limit in-person audiences. Music venues closed again. Performing musicians found themselves scrambling for employment. By this time some had already found other work in nonmusical areas. Others were able to cobble together outdoor programs during the warm weather or offer internet alternatives. Almost any place could become a performance venue.

What Do Money and Stage Fright Have in Common?

Without getting too graphic, it should be recalled that Freud famously argued for a connection between money and certain products of the body—since young children view potty training as a way to give "gifts" to caregivers.[5] Thus there is some reason to think that children learn to think of money as "dirty" and associate different kinds of performances with their ability to control their bodies in a satisfactory way. Music, too, is expressed through performers' bodies and minds through technique and sensitive interpretations as performers produce interesting things. What may be felt and dreaded as humiliation in relation to musical performances can be rooted deeply in unconscious mental functions that underlie this connection between money, bodily control, and making music.

In this context, we can think about some common expressions used by musicians who feel they have displayed inadequate technique or had memory slips on their instruments. Performers typically deride themselves for "dropping too many notes" or "messing up" performances, metaphorically suggesting the idea of losing something of bodily value (technique) and emotional value (musical interpretations) in front of the public. After all, technique and memory slips are mental and biological functions that originate inside the physical body and are very often inhibited through debilitating stage fright suffered by many performers. *The fear is great that they will feel humiliated and the audience will laugh, walk out, and, worst of all, withdraw love (a primal fear that intensifies stage fright).*

In my clinical work with performers, I have observed that the emotions of shame and humiliation are inhibiting, painful, and debilitating for performers' egos and generate intense anxiety and self-doubt. The body and mind malfunctioned in public. Performances cannot be perfect. Musicians probably will "drop notes" and make "technical messes or boo-boos" onstage. These occurrences leave performers feeling humiliated and full of shame and blatantly exposed in public. The emotional consequences of feeling lacking and ineffective are searing and reach back into early-childhood experiences about making sandcastles and mud pies.

Linda

Linda entered music school with the intent of a performance career when she graduated. While she found employment in low-paying jobs after graduation with an undergraduate degree in violin, she was unable to sustain herself for long, always searching for temporary positions until she was successful in finding either teaching or orchestra work. She earned her living by working two nonmusic jobs. Linda decided to accept a well-paying position in a start-up company. The compensation was quite good but she found herself bored and unhappy without music. She returned to graduate school for further music study—but felt older than and in competition with younger students. Her parents continued to question her spending more money to risk unemployment with another degree. She pressured herself to play with technical proficiency with little ability to tolerate any mistakes and felt terrible if performances and auditions did not go "perfectly." She became more despondent and anxious about what she would do with two degrees in music and no steady job in music that paid a decent salary.

Eventually and somewhat reluctantly, she called me to schedule some sessions, and after a great deal of self-reflection, she found a job in a more administrative capacity in an arts organization, played chamber music at weddings and special events, and began to teach music lessons privately. She became less demanding of herself and found she could use her music to find pleasure, earn a living, and share her gift with others in numerous ways. She realized, over time, that she needed to diversify her interests and talent.

For many people, the metaphors that link money, love, dirt, and messes (unconsciously, until discovered in therapy when exploring the use of specific words that describe feelings) may feel far-fetched and even weird. For therapists who help patients look beneath the surface of their overt distress (as a musician would probe the counterpoint or harmony beneath a melody), it is not unusual to hear musicians use phrases of everyday speech about how they "messed up" and "had an accident" (a memory or technical slip musically. Musicians fear similar humiliating memory-slip situations of forgetting the music performing before the public.

Exploring various multiply-determined ways to conceptualize money can expand our thinking and understanding about why money tends to be a taboo and often uncomfortable topic. Money can be implicated more specifically in performers' emphasis about giving "clean" or "note-perfect" performances, which in turn bring desired bravissimos as rewards—but often not much money.

How Much Are You Worth?

Money stimulates fantasies regarding our self-worth, how we think about ourselves, and how we interact with others. Exchanges of psychic income for performances and services occur between performers and audiences, producers and organizers, and teachers and students. Money can satisfy and represent a basic human need to feel valued and worthwhile. Money can represent power and success. Money also can evoke misery and failure. Money can represent dependence or independence and validate self-concept. For some, money defines their sense of self or society's endorsement or lack of endorsement of their "products." Musicians are their own "products," and the topic of their value is experienced very personally and viscerally—both through joy and through shame.

Money begins sending signals to aspiring musicians at a young age. Interestingly, many families are supportive of their talented children, pay large amounts of money for instruments and lessons, and are proud to show off their young prodigious progenies. Yet as the creative adolescents and young adults profess a desire to make music a serious profession, doubts and reservations are expressed by the families about the practicality and advisability of making music a serious career choice. Money is implicitly implicated if not explicitly stated in these messages. If the career path is endorsed, rousing send-offs to music schools or conservatories can be loaded with mixed messages and awaken conflict for the young serious musicians (who may already be unconsciously aware of the risks of making a good-enough living through music). Fantasies of "stardom" or "my career will be the exception" are not uncommon, which avoid or dilute the need to think of money more practically. For those who aspire to a music career other than performance, awareness of the financial challenges of economic disparities for musicians in multiple roles also is suggested.

Patrons and Angels

Some classical composers, such as Bach, Mozart, Beethoven, and Haydn, found favor from wealthy patrons, churches, or courts to fund their work. Mozart was famously kicked out by his patron, the archbishop of Salzburg, for his sassy, impudent behavior. One wonders if Mozart's need for dependency and search for a father figure who would pay him with love and not demand his earnings (as did Leopold) played a role here.[6] Pyotr Ilyich Tchaikovsky was financed by a wealthy widow. The government of Finland supported Jean Sibelius for life. Angela Coolidge commissioned works of Béla Bartók, Benjamin Britten, Maurice Ravel, and Igor Stravinsky. Aaron Copland's ballet *Appalachian Spring* was made possible by the Coolidge Foundation.[7]

Not all musicians are lucky enough to find an "angel" or a perfect mother or father, but that does not deter them from hoping to find support or have it find them. Since musicians are so personally identified with their work and career choice, it would be curious indeed if money did *not* hold significant meaning in their sense of self and feeling "wanted and appreciated." Psychic income is only a more obvious part of the story. What is a musician's value to himself or herself? Do some musicians feel deserving? Do some both fear and seek dependency, ashamed about negotiating fees for fear of being annoyingly demanding or offensive or, worse, of receiving no invitations at all (i.e., of basic nutritional sources as represented by the mother's life-saving nurturance, now projected onto audience and producer approval, being totally denied)? Professing "I love what I do" and "I love to be a musician" without attaching a dollar amount for the transaction of talent, preparation, and "musical services" produces a monetary and psychological conundrum—and neglects the reality of earning "real" dollars while not exploring a deeper issue of self-concept and one's worth.

Buying Love

The Beatles sang about a deeper meaning of money in their iconic song "Can't Buy Me Love." For some performers, buying love means giving freely (apparently the Beatles could give and receive audience love—and money—from their performances). Too often for musicians, applause and repeat invitations become the currency exchanged for services when insufficient fees are offered for impressive programs given (sometimes donated) by talented individuals. Faculty salaries that are typically published at universities make salient the discrepancies between music-school salaries and salaries in other departments. Star faculty members receive substantially higher salaries in both music departments and other divisions.

Literal definitions of words can be misleading. Work is not "play" or frivolous activity for musicians, although we routinely speak of musicians *playing* instruments.[8] A polished performance appears to be effortless due to the unseen, extraordinarily long hours spent practicing and preparing for the public two hours onstage plus years of training beginning in childhood.

Nourishing Starving Artists

Applause is a gratifying reward, but it cannot be deposited in the bank or pay for a new furnace or a car repair. How often have you given a performance for a "small budget" when the host "regretfully" informed you that he or she would "love to have you on the program" but "cannot afford to pay you the appropriate fee that you deserve"? Think about how you have responded—and felt.

We all sometimes donate our talents and our services. Doing this too often makes you a volunteer, not a professional. It also can make you resentful if your choice is to be a professional. Such is the perceived glamor and myth of the "starving artist" who sacrifices everything for work. Such is the trajectory of an underpaid professional, which is neither glamorous nor a myth.

Musicians are often not fully prepared to enter the job market without a rudimentary knowledge of the economics of working in highly competitive, saturated, and underpaid environments. I sometimes wonder how many talented musicians or other people are choked out of the job market due to lack of knowledge about handling economic issues. Institutions that teach serious musicians can assist their students in this conundrum by offering interdisciplinary programs with business schools and inviting financial entrepreneurs as well as well-known performers who are willing to share their experiences and perhaps mentor students about earning living wages after graduation. While concrete problems of economics are discussed in chapter 2, here we have looked closer at the psychological meanings that musicians attach to the economics of their chosen profession. With greater understanding of the deeper meanings of money, musicians can experience both real and psychic income as sources of pleasure and self-worth.

Notes

1. R. Tractman, "The Money Taboo: Its Effects in Everyday Life and in the Practice of Psychotherapy," *Clinical Social Work Journal* 27, no. 3 (Fall 1999): 275–88.

2. D. M. Kaplan, *Clinical and Social Realities*, ed. L. J. Kaplan (Northvale: Jason Aronson Inc., 1995); D. M. Kaplan, "On stage fright," *The Drama Review* 14, no. 1 (1969): 60–83.

3. S. Akhtar, "Normal and Pathological Generosity," *Psychoanal. Review* 99, no. 5 (2012): 671.

4. A. R. Terkel, "Money as a Mirror of Marriage," *Journal of The American Academy of Psychoanalysis* 16, no. 4 (1988): 525–35, https://doi.org/10.1521/jaap.1.1988.16.4.525.

5. S. Freud, "Character and anal erotism," in *The standard edition of the complete psychological works of Sigmund Freud*, vol. 9, ed. and trans. J. Strachey (London: Hogarth Press, 1908), 167–76.

6. Leopold Mozart, a successful violin teacher and demanding father of his genius son, promoted Wolfgang to earn money for the family. Thus the father illustrated dependency on his son.

7. Classic FM, "Who were the great patrons of music - and which pieces would not have existed without them?" First published July 10, 2015. Updated April 12, 2019. https://www.classicfm.com/discover-music/latest/great-patrons-music/.

8. E. S. Bordin, "Fusing work and play: A challenge to theory and research," *Academic Psychology Bulletin* 1 (1979): 5–9; E. S. Bordin, "Work and Play," in *Encyclopedia of Psychology*, vol. 3, ed. R. J. Corsini (New York: John Wiley, 1984), 447–78; E. S. Bordin, "A psychodynamic model of career choice and satisfaction," in *Career Choice and Development*, eds. D. Brown and L. Brooks and Assoc. (San Francisco: Jossey-Bass, 1984).

CHAPTER FIVE

~

Four Types of Personality Who Seek Music Careers

"Who am I?" is a question each of us asks, and the answer differs at each stage of life. The complex concept of identity has proven difficult to understand scientifically, although it importantly contributes to career choice and how we feel about ourselves and toward others. Various psychological and personality tests examine aptitudes and attitudes about career choice. A single test cannot capture the deeper essence of personality or the psychological factors that contribute to occupational choice, however. Erik Erikson's developmental biopsychosocial theory, discussed in chapter 3, can be used to conceptualize occupational choice in musicians in the context of human development. His theory is used here to make sense of some empirical data about a select population of young adults who are in the process of making choices about their careers in music.

Even a sophisticated protocol such as this one cannot predict or be used in isolation from more comprehensive assessments, which also were used in the research to be reported. I pick out some important information based on the Identity Status Interview protocol to emphasize distinct differences and some similarities among musicians who are in the process of making a career decision, with a special focus on the period of identity consolidation during late adolescence and young-adulthood.

The Identity Status Interview

While the study of personality includes issues other than occupational choice, the nexus of one's personal identity is related closely to this decision.

The Identity Status Interview (ISI) provides one way to concretize and think about this momentous commitment. The ISI was developed by psychologist James Marcia in 1966.[1] His model for assessing occupational choice and personal identity remains relevant in current research about a variety of professions and life choices. I am using it here to share my research with young adults and clinical findings about significant underlying issues that contribute to the choice of a career in music. Some of these people pursued their choice in music; others eventually gravitated in different directions.[2]

The ISI suggests that emotional conflict around decisions regarding career choice in older adolescents and young adults reflects four basic types of decision-making. This Interview, when applied to musicians, is compatible with Erikson's work on the solidification of identity during the developmental stages of the young adult, which bridge childhood and adolescence into adulthood and culminate in career choice. The ISI statistically analyzes attributes and attitudes of individuals who are drawn to their occupation and correlates the data with more informal and subjective interviews and other tools. The profiles are striking, and you may recognize yourself in one, or several, of them.

The Four Categories of the ISI

According to the ISI, decisions regarding career choice fall into one of four categories: achieved, foreclosed, moratorium, and diffused.

Identity Achieved

Identity Achieved individuals seek a career in music (performance) but have tried or thought seriously about other occupational options. They have weighed the pros and cons of their decision. Ultimately, they have arrived at their choice, perhaps despite parental objections, and, most importantly, are relatively conflict-free and assured about what they want to pursue.

Identity Foreclosed

Identity Foreclosed individuals, similar to Identity Achieved, maintain that a career in music is their goal. However, these people, unlike the Achieved musicians, never have considered career alternatives. Generally, they are following a career path or lifestyle that is approved and encouraged by their parents. Their self-esteem is greatly dependent upon approval by authority figures, who include parents, teachers, and audiences.

Identity Moratorium

Identity Moratorium individuals are musicians currently in crisis about their career plans. Undecided and weighing numerous alternatives, these individuals are considering their talent, their potential, parental opinions, and the social and economic problems that confront musicians. They are having difficulty making a choice.

Identity Diffused

Identity Diffused individuals may pursue music professionally because they enjoy music and the attention performance brings or the satisfaction teaching offers. They also feel other professions offer satisfaction. They have not explored any particulars about what musicians "do," and their smorgasbord attitude of "everything looks good" reflects a lack of commitment to any particular choice as well as a lack of struggle. They appear to have a day-to-day chameleon-like attitude.

What Does ISI Data Explain?

The ISI provides a useful snapshot of individuals at a particular moment in their psychological development when making a momentous life decision—a moment underpinned by earlier developmental stages embedded in adolescent and young-adult experiences. The ISI can shed significant insight on the process that is involved in making music a career and a life choice. In the discussion that follows, I refer to data drawn from both quantitative sources (questionnaires) and qualitative sources (live interviews). Information was gathered from advanced music performance majors enrolled in a major university music program. A selection of the data analysis is summarized.[3] The data were evaluated for reliability and validity and are representative of the individuals who were part of this study. Selected relevant results are noted below.

- Achieved and Foreclosed individuals appeared similar in their professed certainty about career choice.
- Foreclosed individuals were more defensive about their feelings than seemed apparent on the surface and were motivated primarily by family expectations.
- Achieved individuals had sufficiently worked through troublesome family issues and conflicts, often trying other career interests before deciding upon music. They scored low in stage fright.

- Moratorium individuals who were experiencing crisis and were uncommitted and
- Diffused individuals were higher in performance anxiety.
- Females reported higher performance anxiety than males.[4]
- Performance anxiety was a frequently stated reason career choices in music were abandoned or redirected.

A Foreclosed female said playing the piano in public was "probably the worst experiences of my life. A lot of people say that as soon as they start performing, it [performance anxiety] gets better. Not me. When I play a piano solo I go crazy the entire time. All I'm thinking about is getting those notes finished. I wish I had decided to major in another subject."

By contrast, an Achieved male who was committed to his music career described performing as follows: "I try to stand backstage and tell myself that, OK, you've got something people want to see, and I sort of psych myself out. Usually I am nervous when I first start, but then after you're out there you lose yourself if you get involved enough in what you're doing so you're not thinking about what the audience is thinking. You're thinking about what you're doing."

While practicing an instrument alone for hours may be adaptive for young musicians whose home lives are in turmoil, adult musicians suffer, often emotionally and physically, if underlying issues are not addressed. Career choice and stage fright are related where performance anxiety is a symptom of unresolved underlying issues from one's early years.

A Moratorium female spoke of debilitating stage fright in her interview: "My parents were divorced and my mother kept reminding me that musicians didn't get jobs. . . . She told me to go into the sciences. It made me mad, but I also got a little scared. My mother was afraid I would leave her to live with my father and she resented any contact with my father. . . . She made me promise I wouldn't leave. I always resented all of that. We had horrible fights when I came home from college on vacation. I also resented my father for leaving. He did nothing to send me through college. Now I have sixty thousand dollars debt in loans to pay back. I just resent him."

These data and examples do not prove that musicians either work through or play through earlier domestic turmoil and feelings. They give snapshots of musicians frozen in the time frame of interviews or questionnaires. Clinical data add to the picture. Clinical experiences treating anxious musicians and research data offered here both suggest more strongly that there is higher debilitating anxiety in those musicians who love music and desire a career in it but find difficulty coping with intense unexamined internal stress that expresses itself as performance anxiety. This is similar to the experiences of my patients who are not in the performing arts but who strive to do their jobs "right" or "perfectly." Their pursuit of perfection never permits them to feel reliably gratified or appreciated by their extraordinarily harsh and demanding consciences.[5]

It is not unusual, as the Moratorium young woman stated, for anger to be mixed with guilt over feeling resentful and angry at parents and others. Unresolved anger, often fueled by shame and guilt that underlie it, has the power consciously and unconsciously to undermine talent. Anger also can appear in disguised symptoms of stage fright. This, in turn, can sabotage the most talented and prepared musicians (and other professionals) who are at the pivotal point of making (or already having made) a vocational choice. This is particularly salient when that choice is conflicted. These data further illustrate that stage fright is not "*the* problem" but is a symptom of underlying issues and feelings that emerged during an earlier stage in life before occupational choices and identity were identified, much less solidified. A brief clinical example illustrates a connection between anger, performance anxiety, and career choice.

Ken: Integrating Past and Present

Ken called for an appointment to see me following what he described as a "disastrous performance." He told me that he had ruined his recent concert, during which he had sloppy technique and memory slips throughout the program. He noted this was occurring more frequently, and while he had resisted seeing a therapist and tried to solve things himself, he finally allowed himself to call for help.

At our first meeting, Ken told me that it had been difficult to ask for help and he had put it off for a long time. His parents had told him that "smart people solved their own problems." Also, he grew up in a family that maintained people who needed to see "shrinks" were crazy. I responded that it must have been difficult to call me since he had heard that people who sought out care for emotional issues were both crazy and dumb. I told him I did not think he was either but understood how it was difficult to acknowledge that he could benefit from help.

Ken told me that his parents did not want him to go into music for his career, although he had loved playing the cello seriously since junior high school. He had been successful in several competitions both in high school and in college, where he found he enjoyed being around people who felt as passionate about music as he did. He told me that he found the cello soothing as an adolescent when his father yelled at him and that he always feared being punished if he did not conform to what was expected. Although he tried to gain favor with his father, he never lived up to what was asked. It became clear that his self-esteem was blunted and his self-confidence in performing in public was severely compromised—not by his talent but by his self-image and fear of displeasing teachers and disappointing conductors (both of who were displacements of his father). At the time he called me, he feared that he would be yelled at by the conductor if he continued to make mistakes.

Ken gradually started to talk about his family and revealed more concerns about his career choice. He started to develop a pain in his bow arm at this time in our work. He feared he would have to give up music altogether, and he started looking up career options online and talking with others who were not in music. He contemplated seeing a career coach and started to visit numerous physicians to find a diagnosis and relief for his pain. He hoped he could benefit from physical treatment, but if not, he would decide to abandon music altogether. He also started to tell me that he was starting to doubt that "just talking" with me would help him very much. After many visits with doctors, he never received a diagnosis because no doctor could find any medical abnormality. I asked him if he could think more about his emotions and feelings to try to discover how his mind and body were telling him something through his pain and his anxiety about continuing in music—or not.

According to ISI criteria, Ken was a Foreclosed musician—wanting music for a career but also fearful of not pleasing his parents, who objected, and also his conductor, his audiences, and me, his therapist. Ken also told me he had a dream that his girlfriend left him and when he woke up he was surprised she was still with him. Through his associations, we learned that he feared I would leave him because he was angry with me and doubted I could help—as he had felt with his parents.

Over the course of many sessions, we learned not only that Ken had been afraid of his father and his father's temper—which had led to physical abuse at times—but also that Ken was afraid of his own temper. He also was frightened of being too good at the cello because that would clearly upset his father even as it advanced his own career goals.

As I tried to put some pieces together to help Ken, I noted that I thought he was telling us that he was angry about his father's attitude about music and also fearful of his father's temper. I asked if he might also fear his own anger and fear what would happen if it got out of control, like his music technique—and that perhaps he would yell or even hit someone with his arm that had begun to hurt. I wondered if he worried he would lash out at me. I added that if his arm hurt too badly, he could not use it to strike out—or play his cello. Ken became pensive and quiet. Tears welled up, which he would not allow to flow in my presence. Following a poignant silence, I noted his sadness as though he was feeling something important and experiencing it deeply.

Subsequent sessions allowed us to understand how his performance anxiety was related to many issues he brought to the stage and to his relationships. These feelings would not allow him to express himself verbally or musically. Over time, Ken worked to integrate his past and present and make some decisions for himself that felt right and guilt free. He enjoyed playing his cello and his arm did not ache. We came to the realization that his heart was aching for the love from his father that he believed was not forthcoming. Making music when we first met soothed his pain but it came with anxiety and anger attached to it—a high price to pay. Ken resumed his music ambitions and found pleasure in doing so. He no longer needed to feel pain in his arm or worry he would act upon his anger. He was able to make greater peace with his past and look forward to a future making a contribution in music.

When I think about Ken now some years after we ended our work, I hear elements of all four of the Identity Status categories. He wanted to be a musician and also had thought about and briefly tried alternatives (Achieved). He wanted to please his parents and receive their love, but his father disapproved of his career choice and mistreated him, which escalated anxiety (Foreclosed). He was almost ready to leave music but was ambivalent about doing it when he called me to help with his dilemma with performance anxiety and physical pain (Moratorium). He had begun to explore other options and tried a couple jobs temporarily but vacillated back and forth as everything felt good but nothing felt "right." Ken could not solve his ambivalence about making a career choice either in or away from music (Diffused). He felt anxious and stuck.

Conclusion: Research and Clinical Work

A well-constructed research design can identify distinct variables and place findings into discrete categories, while clinical evidence addresses the complexity of developmental and personality issues that are represented by mental and physical symptoms such as performance anxiety.

When a person's conflicted wishes or decisions that affect career satisfaction evoke strong feelings, it is important to understand this dilemma in the context of a whole person who brings a personal history to treatment. I believe that Ken, for instance, was helped with his presenting dilemma, performance anxiety, through allowing himself to look at performance anxiety as a clue to see his distress in a broader context and ultimately to solidify his identity and discover and explore multiple underlying emotions that contributed to his symptoms. Our therapeutic explorations of his distress and the professional relationship that developed between us allowed Ken to make adaptive future decisions that felt right for himself without suffering from debilitating guilt and anger.

Notes

1. J. E. Marcia, "Development and validation of ego-identity status," *Journal of Personality and Social Psychology* 3 (1966): 551–58.

2. Marcia's early research was conducted with male subjects. Subsequent studies found no gender differences between males and females in identity status. See J. E. Marcia and M. L. Friedman, "Ego identity status in college women," *Journal of Personality* 38, no. 2 (1970): 249–63; M. H. Podd, J. E. Marcia, and B. M. Rubin, "The effects of ego identity and partner perception on a prisoner's dilemma game," *Journal of Social Psychology* 83 (1970): 117–26.

3. For more detail, see J. J. Nagel, "An Examination Commitment to Careers in Music: Implications for Alienation from Vocational Choice" (unpublished doctoral dissertation, Psychology and Social Work, University of Michigan, 1987), Dissertation Abstracts International, 42, 5-A, 1154–1155.

4. It is unclear if women reveal their feelings more freely than men which leads to the data that show they experience higher performance anxiety.

5. Most published research on performance anxiety with musicians has been conducted in a cognitive behavioral model. A psychodynamic perspective on performance anxiety is less represented in the literature. These two paradigms are significantly different in their approaches to theory and treatment. Behavioral theory and treatment is focused upon symptom removal, whereas psychodynamic theories and treatment considers the whole person in the context of developmental precedents and helps people better understand why they think and feel as they do. This approach leads to symptom resolution and understanding of underlying motives. In all cases, a thorough evaluation must be conducted with a prospective patient.

CHAPTER SIX

~

Pursuit of Perfection

The pursuit of "perfection" is observed in many ambitious people and notably in a number of musicians. As in sports, being number one and winning love and admiration are challenges to be conquered. The wish to be number one also is related to psychological issues other than performance itself. Musicians or athletes or business executives, teachers, office workers, or supervisors attempt to achieve a sense of control, uniqueness, and specialness, as children long to feel with parents. Frequently I have heard patients talk about their efforts to "change" other people if the patients figure out how to "do or say what is right" and thereby acquire "perfect love and approval." Perfection often is emphasized as "the answer" at the expense of examining what fuels underlying emotional pressures that these feelings place upon individuals. There is tenacity to a magic belief, hearkening back to childhood magic (discussed in chapter 3). Figuring out how to be "perfect," it is assumed, will lead to a satisfying and illustrious career.

The pursuit of perfection among musicians is understandable. Careers in music *are* notoriously competitive, demand high standards, and require years of study. Winning competitions in school and locally, nationally, and internationally often *is* an entry ritual to gaining a foothold in a highly competitive music arena. It is unfortunate that music competitions, traditionally a pathway to a career or at least gaining fame, choose one person as winner among a field of enormously talented individuals. This leaves many other talented musicians disappointed and unrecognized backstage and off-stage. Losing an audition or being rejected for a job (perhaps with several hundred talented people applying for one open position) intensifies feel-ings of loss or incompetence. Developmentally, love and approval are basic needs from earlier ages that appear in competitive situations throughout life. Feelings of rejection cannot be ignored or overcome by practicing longer or networking harder. These feelings hurt! Losing *is* disappointing! When talented individuals are thrust into a highly competitive and evaluative atmosphere, stressors from earlier years are reactivated and can turn into psychological pressure cookers. The quest for perfection as a "solution" is not effective but often is not given up easily either. Rather, this "try harder" pressure often intensifies self-doubt, comparison with others, and disillu-sionment. Such feelings undermine talent based on "perfectionism anxiety" and often are thinly camouflaged as performance anxiety.

Many talented musicians arrive at universities or conservatories without exploring perfectionistic wishes or career alternatives. Early attraction and specialization on an instrument that evolves into the pursuit of a career in music can narrow thinking about nonmusical or blended creative alterna-tives. It did for me. After I completed geometry in high school, I did not take additional math courses because I "knew" I was going to be in music and would not need advanced math . . . or so I thought then. I found myself back in graduate school years later and was required to take graduate statistics. I was totally flummoxed until I realized how my music training had prepared me to work hard and analyze a different kind of "data" called notes, rhythms, melodies, and formal structures. Gradually I understood that the abstract, nonverbal language of statistics was not so different.

One cannot start to decide to become a professional musician at the age of sixteen or eighteen or twenty-five. Yet one *can* decide *after* becoming a mu-sician to modulate to another career (or expand one's chosen occupation). With jobs in the musical arts so scarce, financial remuneration typically inadequate, and competition fierce, it is imperative today that music educa-tors ask, "How can we best train talented young people?" The pandemic has taught us that we cannot narrowly pursue music careers that were imagin-able, even if difficult to establish and maintain, just five years ago. The words of my high school choir teacher reverberate: "Keep your options open."

The Disillusionment of Omnipotence

How ironic that a career that promises considerable intrinsic gratification for musicians also contains a "catch-22." The "escape" from family situa-tions for some people is provided by emotional and technical investment in an instrument combined with fantasies of a glamorous career. There is a fantasy that this career may fulfill daydreams of bravos and audience love. Conversely, the immersion in music study at an early age, encouraged or discouraged by families, may hold devastating disappointment. The realities typically become salient only after many years have been invested working toward a music career.

For individuals who pursue a music career against parental endorsement, anxiety and guilt may surface as the musicians begin to experience self-doubt, as we read in the discussion about Ken in chapter 5. There is a need to prove parents wrong. Anxiety over displeasing parents and losing their love often becomes displaced onto others and projected onto the audience, teachers, and therapists. Career choice becomes conflicted, tarnished, and dimmed with performance anxiety, self-doubt, or depression, which cloud the musicians' dreams. This scenario has the potential to sabotage the pursuit of "perfection," which speaks to issues deeper than playing wrong notes and stumbling through embarrassing memory slips. The realization that there is *no such thing as perfection* can feel like a relief but also a punch in the gut. How do talented and highly trained musicians cope with this harsh wake-up call?

On the other extreme, zealous parents who may be involved vicariously in their offspring's music endeavors (perhaps to fill gaps of their own wishes and less-than-realized professional aspirations—musical or otherwise) also may have detrimental effects. Young musicians attempt to disentangle from childhood relationships in traversing a second version of individuation. This potentially stormy and exciting period of life is adolescents' version of toddlers' separation-individuation phase.[1] Marcia suggests that "perfect" parents may be stifling as well as luxuriant.[2] Margaret Mahler comments, "Growing up entails a gradual growing away from the normal state of human symbiosis, of 'one-ness' with the mother. This process is much slower in the emotional and psychic area than in the physical one."[3] As such, there is a loss of an idealized relationship. Stepping toward or away from parental wishes is daunting when developing one's own identity and actualizing one's own wishes. It is not difficult to understand that the pursuit of perfection is an impossible developmental task to actualize.

When individuals have avoided confronting difficult psychological issues and find themselves in a highly competitive and evaluative environment, stress can sabotage illusions of "perfection" in the pursuit of a music career. Reality eventually replaces fantasies that, nevertheless, doggedly perpetuate this omnipotent illusion as a solution.[4] Often, pessimism dilutes optimism. Disillusionment darkens illusions, although it never extinguishes them entirely. One can always wish upon a star—or wish to become one.

The relationship between music performers and audiences—like the musicians' relationship with music itself—is unique. This performer-music-audience relationship offers the opportunity for musicians to express wishes, hopes, fears, and other fantasies about the public, who become metaphorically experienced as parental substitutes. Each individual is constitutionally and psychologically unique and sees the world through personally constructed filters. Parents provide the most important blueprint for later life. Both illusions and disillusionment plant roots in our earliest years.

People act and feel, both knowingly and unknowingly, in ways that attempt to replicate or compensate for infant and childhood relationships, gains, and losses. Thus, the original parent-child relationship, which evokes the nurturing and appreciative (or sometimes distant) caretaker, is ever present and becomes repeated—often through career choice. Recall Erik Erikson's developmental stages in chapter 3 in which each stage of biopsychosocial experience becomes folded into subsequent stages throughout life.

When basic needs of care and love are met sufficiently for infants or toddlers, the children are more likely to develop trust and confidence that as performers they will be able to evoke nurturing responses from others. Musical offerings originally begin as gurgles and coos in the nursery, and in childhood, "magic thinking" convinces young children that they have an effect on others who will fulfill their wishes. Early parent-child interactions provide the basis for a sense of competence and the roots for self-esteem. Feeling competent and confident helps one overcome adversity when necessary as well as provides sufficient confidence on the music podium and on the stage of life.

Growing Pains and Emotional Growth

Trauma and unavoidable changes that may occur during the early years, such as illness, divorce, death of loved ones, birth of siblings, and relocations in the family, can upset idyllic equilibrium. Some children, due to genetic or biological factors, are not easily soothed, despite the best efforts of caregivers. Parents also have needs and worries of their own with which they cope. Over time, all children are forced to acknowledge that they are not the "center of the universe with the power to make everyone meet all needs."[5] Attunement between parents and children, despite best efforts, may become dissonant. Parents may not, despite intentions, always be able to provide comfort, reassurance, and gratification to their children.

Children typically become disillusioned and angry with Paradise Lost, which can linger unconsciously in the mind. Longings for Paradise Found can be played out over the course of a lifetime, often in ways that seem unconnected and unremembered in response to earlier disappointments, experienced as slight or major losses. Young children's concrete solutions explain what they cannot understand, as discussed in chapter 3. The process of self-reflection and reevaluating unexamined "truths" is arduous. To give up an old belief (which involves emotional readjustments), even when that belief repeatedly does not work (such as practicing a difficult passage over and over and over—*the same way*), is painful and frightening.

Communication between people with separate personalities and needs can have far-reaching consequences, particularly when miscommunications become problematic and remain unresolved. Developmentally, young children internalize feelings of not being responded to as a threat to feeling competent, which plummets the children into diminished self-esteem. For some people, a conviction that *"if* I can be perfect—as a child, parent, musician, etc.—*then* other people will love me and understand me and provide what I want." The impossible quest for perfection is set in motion, accompanied by a painful sense of disappointment, incompetence, and helplessness and low self-esteem. The growing realization of the impossibility of perfection causes a loss of young children's sense of being invincible or masters of the universe. More realistic challenges of being "human" are lessons to be learned and absorbed over a lifetime. A belief in one's competence also can grow stronger so that one does not feel impaired, insulted, criticized, or angry when one falls short of perfection. One need not try ever harder to be perfect in order to be loved—or hired.

All individuals, not only musicians, face painful losses of ideals, loved ones, and special friends. Fast-forwarding from childhood, musicians seek out audiences, teachers, mentors, friends, and therapists to establish meaningful relationships. Each new relationship has the potential to perpetuate the hope and fantasy that there is a good-enough person available to fill the gap left from childhood disappointments. Sturdy self-esteem, even during times of doubt, can help mitigate the need to become overly reliant on others, such as audiences and teachers, as the primary (or only) source of ego enhancement.

The quest for "perfection" can result in an emotional dead end and impede a basic human need for appreciation and love. A search for competence can be sabotaged psychologically as the illusion of perfection turns disillusionment into self-deprecation. These beliefs about oneself erode self-appreciation. When self-esteem withers and anxiety increases, a deeper examination of psychological conflicts with a trained professional will be invaluable. Career goals may be realized or readjusted without being disbanded altogether as they become understood in a broader context that puts "perfection" into a realistic perspective rather than an all-or-nothing requirement.

Pursuit of Perfection: All the Right Notes

Not surprisingly, the pursuit of perfection can create anxiety around musicians' relationships with career choice. When does a quest for "perfection" become debilitating, illusory, and self-destructive? How does this demanding work ethic affect performers' identities? What is perfection anyway?

Musicians' self-doubts often are centered concretely upon their perceived sloppy technique and inferior interpretive ability. It is not unusual for performers to demand an extraordinarily high standard for themselves which prohibits making any (perceived or actual) mistakes in public. Not surprisingly, this impossible fantasy about being perfect, as though there is a devastating flaw in one's personality, serves to escalate tension, fuels low self-esteem, and leads to high levels of stage fright.

The quest for the illusion of being flawless can undermine talent; but more so, it diminishes the joy gained from making and sharing music. This arduous search for perfection can be experienced in a variety of emotional and physically related problems expressed by musicians.[6] My emphasis here is that our inner tensions and exacting demands upon ourselves evolve long before we walk onstage or into a classroom. They have a significant history and a stubborn trajectory that may adversely affect our feelings about our competence and eventually undermine it when nothing less than "perfection" is the gold standard.

While the study of personality includes issues other than occupational choice, the nexus of one's personal identity appears to be related closely to our attitudes about work and how we exert pressures upon ourselves. Research indicates dissonance and doubts exist in career choice for numerous performing musicians (e.g., indecision, rejection, wrestling with vocational alternatives, physical complaints, and debilitating stage fright).[7] Despite many years of study and preparation, musicians are negatively affected by self-doubt, stage fright, and problematic economic conditions when they place perfectionistic pressure upon themselves.

Ms. G

Ms. G's concerns about her music performance anxiety were painful but not unusual (fear of insecure memory and inadequate technique). She was obsessively determined to practice long hours every day in order to play "all the right notes." She became increasingly frustrated that she could not be "perfect on or off stage." A disappointing performance that she called "disastrous" led her to call me to schedule an appointment.

I discovered quickly that she demanded I become her "perfect" therapist with all the right answers (i.e., that I play all the "right notes" or say the "right thing") for her. She showed great concern about "what I thought" about her as her therapist, as though through displacement I was her audience. She often felt criticized by me and by others although she most severely disparaged herself. Her anxiety often escalated to panic. Ms. G resisted examining her emotional life and revisiting some painful feelings and relationships that originated in her childhood which were exacerbated when making her career choice in music.

Our work helped her realize that what she could gain from me was imperfect but tolerable and often helpful. She did not have to try to please me to gain my respect. Ms. G gradually started to realize her need for "others" to be perfect was a projection of her own feelings of incompetence that she projected onto them because she was so demanding of herself. Over time, she realized that she could appreciate that she was a competent person who was more than a musician (or a magician) who must play "all the right notes" when she put impossible pressures upon herself. She eventually made a truce with her inner perfectionistic demons and was then able to make peace emotionally with a more accepting attitude toward herself and about her career choice. Ms. G started to find satisfaction in her career choice.

Mr. D

Mr. D could not decide whether to stay in music or find another career. He approached and avoided treatment as he did music and other jobs he tried briefly but abandoned. He could not give up music nor could he follow through with any other plans. In his relationships he reenacted his earlier experience of being abandoned emotionally by his parents, who divorced after many arguments that he overheard as a child. He insisted he had caused their rupture because he was not the "perfect" son. Music was the only thing that soothed his anxiety when he felt unhappy or guilty.

When he believed he played well, he felt secure and wonderful. If his playing did not go exceptionally well (in his opinion), he said he "felt ill." Contrary to my inviting him to say anything that was on his mind, he tried to say the "right thing." Yet he was afraid if he and I did not think in unison that we would argue, like his parents. He repeatedly expressed his worry that his work in therapy was never going to be "perfect" enough to keep me interested in him or helping him. He could not imagine that I wanted to help him see that his worries were not going to be enacted by me or that anger was an acceptable and discussable feeling, related to feeling bereft when his parents divorced. It became clear that he was terrified I would leave him, reenacting his childhood trauma.

One day he did not show up for our appointment. He never called to cancel or reschedule. He did not reply to my attempts to reach him. He recently had told me that he had "forgotten" to buy his mother a Mother's Day card. I do not think it was an accident that his abrupt departure from therapy occurred during the week after Mother's Day. I think he was becoming afraid of warmer feelings and closeness with me. He needed to leave me before (he believed) I would leave him.

Resolution of Disillusionment: Grieving, Mourning, and Moving Forward

Young children's fantasies of being special with the power to have all wishes gratified is abruptly interrupted as maturing young people are forced to delay instant gratification.[8] When sounds (verbal and musical) are no longer concretely perceived as "magic," children have to relinquish the metaphorical throne of "His Majesty the Baby."[9] With increasing maturity, reality becomes a necessity to embrace along with adjusting to empathize with imperfect others, delay gratification, and ultimately find acceptance of one's imperfect self. The illusion of forcing audiences, teachers, friends, or therapists to respond with adoration like parents for dependent children morphs into the reality that this is not always possible and is not a reflection of badness. The power of childhood magic cannot be underestimated or overstated. "Life" deals narcissistic blows after the nursery as development marches forward with new psychological challenges. A recurring dream reported by musicians is that of appearing naked and exposed onstage and feeling ashamed and inadequate. Vulnerability is a prominent feature embedded in this fear. Thus the wish persists, for some, that stellar performances will confirm perfection to alleviate shame and abandonment.

Since musicians' quests for "perfection" are neither realistic nor magic, the resolution of emotional conflicts that swirl around this unattainable goal involve becoming more in tune and more comfortable with one's unique attributes and talent. We are healthiest and more secure psychologically when we realize our selves are not primarily defined by our wishes, by others, or by our work. We develop heartier inner resources when we deeply appreciate ourselves. A full range of emotions is available in musicians' mental repertoire. This repertoire requires hard work and often a painful relinquishing of illusions to cope with the loss of magic wishes and persistent demands from when we believed originally that all things *were* possible.

There is a positive trade-off for loosening the bonds of fantasies of omnipotence. It is empowering to relinquish the helplessness and absolute dependency on others that is necessary and immediately gratifying in infancy. Maturing (and seeking out professional psychological treatment when feeling stuck) helps musicians accept limitations and find fresh ways to create satisfying career plans. This is important "work" for musicians—indeed, for all of us. This process of rediscovery requires making peace with infant and childhood losses, mourning perfectionistic fantasies that cannot be attained, and accepting the disillusionment of our omnipotence, i.e., that everything we want is possible if we only try hard enough or are "perfect" enough. Through grieving "for the small child he once was, he confronts at last the reality of just how starved that small child was for recognition, understanding, and appreciation" and "accepts that things were as they were and are as they are, even if he has wished that they could be otherwise."[10] The mature hope that results from the experience of mastering disillusionment has to do with attaining something that is realizable . . . and experiencing reality as it is . . . and a capacity to experience things anew.[11]

The reality of being human includes strong and contradictory feelings as well as appreciation and tolerance of our own and others' strengths and vulnerabilities. Mourning is an internal response to cope with changes and loosening the idealization and repetition of earliest persistent fantasies of perfection. Mourning involves a painful loss of a wishful fantasy that forces us to courageously examine our deepest longings. We gradually come to terms with our limitations and our assets while exploring our strengths to find pleasure in our talents. These realizations, rather than clinging to the fantasy of achieving omnipotence through perfection, help provide musicians tickets to productive and creative careers. These realizations about disillusionment and the calamities brought by COVID-19 are essential now, particularly in the context of establishing and enjoying career choices in music beyond the pandemic.

Notes

1. P. Blos, *On Adolescence. A Psychoanalytic Interpretation* (New York: The Free Press, 1962).

2. J. E. Marcia, "Identity in Adolescence," in *Handbook of Adolescent Psychology,* ed. Adelson (New York: John Wiley and Sons, 1980).

3. M. S. Mahler, "On the First Three Subphases of the Separation-Individuation Process," *International Journal of Psychoanalysis* 53 (1972): 333–38.

4. I thank Jack and Kerry Kelly Novick for their work on omnipotence and competence which has influenced my thinking.

5. J. Novick and K. K. Novick, "Some comments on masochism and the delusion of omnipotence from a developmental perspective," *Journal of the American Psychoanalytic Association* 38 (1991): 307–32; J. Novick and K. K. Novick, *Fearful Symmetry: The Development and Treatment of Sadomasochism* (Northvale: Jason Aronson, Inc., 1996).

6. J. J. Nagel, "In Pursuit of Perfection: Career Choice and Performance Anxiety in Musicians," *Medical Problems of Performing Artists* (1988): 140–45; D. Kenny, *The Psychology of Music Performance Anxiety* (New York: Oxford University, 2007).

7. Nagel, "Examination"; M. Fishbein et al., "The ICSOM Medical Questionnaire," *Senza Sordino* 25, no. 6 (1988):1–8.

8. Novick and Novick, "Some comments."

9. S. Freud, "On Narcissism: An Introduction," in *The Standard Edition of the Complete Psychological Works of Sigmund Freud*. Vol 14., ed. J. Strachey (London: The Hogarth Press and The Institute of Psycho-Analysis, 1914), 91.

10. M. Stark, *Working with Resistance* (Northvale: Jason Aaronson, Inc., 1994), 279.

11. Stark, *Resistance*, 286, 287.

CHAPTER SEVEN

~

The Golden Allure of Celebrity: Reflections on Boundary Crossings in Psychoanalysis and Music

Some years ago, I was driving to a meeting, half-heartedly listening to National Public Radio. My ears perked up when I heard a performer being interviewed about his burgeoning career. I almost stopped my car when he started talking about how much his life in general, and his music aspirations in particular, had been helped greatly by his psychoanalysis.

Who admits in public that they are seeing a psychoanalyst or volunteers deeply personal information on the radio? This musician unselfconsciously spoke of his inner struggles and the benefits of his analysis that made a positive difference in his performing. Toward the end of the interview, the NPR host played several excerpts from his recordings. This performer was brilliant. By this time, I had become mesmerized by a huge talent whose performing I had just heard but whom I had never seen nor heard about. Although I was late to my meeting, I stayed in my car, glued to the radio, until the interview concluded.

Several weeks later I was talking with my psychoanalytic colleague Dr. Stanley Coen, whom I had known for years through collaborations at the American Psychoanalytic Association (APsaA). I mentioned the radio interview, my reaction to it, and my surprise about how open this musician had been about his psychoanalytic experience. We began to explore the idea of inviting the performer to be a guest presenter at a program we would cochair during the next APsaA national meetings. We discussed a format for a program in which he would be interviewed about his career in music but agreed we would not ask him to perform.

I found the performer's email address online and wrote to him to express how much I enjoyed his NPR interview. I introduced myself as a psychoanalyst and a musician. To my surprise, the performer replied quickly and with appreciation. This began an exchange of emails that were friendly and warm. Dr. Coen and I presented our idea to the APsaA program chair, who thought this would be a fine idea for an interesting program.

I asked the performer if he would agree to be interviewed at an APsaA program the following year. I inquired if he was free from concert obligations on the day of the event and if he would, by chance, be in New York on the proposed date. Performers typically are scheduled months or years in advance of their performances, and I was aware that he may not want to be interviewed in front of an audience of psychoanalysts. To our surprise and delight, this musician *was* free, miraculously *was* going to be in New York on the date of the program, and *was* interested in joining us.

My colleague and I felt it would be a wonderful opportunity to blend music performance and psychoanalysis from someone so ebullient and talented and who spoke so eloquently of his experiences with both. I started to listen to his recordings and was moved by them. When consulting his schedule to see where he would be performing during the coming year, I noted he was performing in a city where my daughter lived. I decided to visit her at that time with the idea she and I could attend a concert and perhaps meet him afterward. I emailed him to see if this was agreeable. He suggested where to meet backstage afterward.

His talent and charisma came alive onstage. After multiple curtain calls, my daughter and I went to say hello and ask for his autograph. He greeted us as though we were friends. It felt wonderful to have established this connection with a famous person who had now befriended me, a stranger, so effusively and warmly. We spoke briefly about the upcoming New York meetings. Photos were taken with him, my daughter, and me, and we said goodbye.

Planning for the Big Meeting

Dr. Coen and I got caught up with planning for the meeting, reassuring ourselves that since the performer was not our patient, we were not imposing on him. In fact, we rationalized that the performer felt fine speaking about himself in public. He had done so on public radio and previously in a newspaper article. We felt that we would be making a unique contribution to our psychoanalytic colleagues and hopefully that a broad exposure would also help promote his career.

We were unable to entertain the idea, at the time, that perhaps our fascination with a celebrity had deeper motivations for us. Planning went well and publicity was sent out to conference members about the program. Correspondence continued regularly between the musician and me as the date for the APsaA meetings neared.

Temptations

Dr. Coen has written about the appeal of celebrities to analysts who treat them, and who, at times, become over-involved with their fame, money, and status.[1] Famous people often can be experienced as seductive and can become special to their analysts. If the feelings of the analysts are unexamined, strong affects may lead to actions. Enactments that may take the place of talking can evolve into eroticized boundary violations, derail the treatment, and create pain and lasting psychological harm. This situation often is romanticized in the movies and on TV where patients and analysts fall in love or establish out-of-office relationships. If this happens professionally, we hear about it in gossip among colleagues. It becomes a serious discussion with significant consequences in professional ethics committees and is the topic of psychoanalytic articles.[2] As Coen writes, even when nothing illicit occurs between famous patients and their analysts, temptations can evoke the analysts' narcissistic and unanalyzed needs since "famous people can be charismatic, confident, and exuberant."[3]

Boundary crossing between music teachers and some of their students shares similar dynamics that could lead to abusive enactments. Like working with special patients, teaching talented students and performers can be intoxicating. The combination of drives, defenses, transference, countertransference, and an intimate work setting between two people can be productive but also toxic if unrecognized, unanalyzed, and unchecked, harming both parties.[4]

How often have many of us been drawn into fantasies about celebrities? In the context of musicians highlighted here, fans become "groupies," seek autographs, or, better yet, acquire celebrity endorsements for their work. Students are thrilled to be recruited or invited to study in esteemed teachers' studios, to win music competitions, or to be chosen first chair in orchestra auditions. These special honors provide a huge ego boost and enhance reputations for both students and teachers. How often do musicians, analysts, teachers, and students tend to rate their self-worth predominantly through the approval of others? How many people determine self-worth as it is defined by teaching (or being taught by) or treating (or being treated by) famous "others"?

Students and teachers alike idealize celebrities because of celebrities' charismatic public personae and career reputations, which spawn fantasies about their private lives. Both teachers and students may be looking for a "special someone" emotionally or physically in their current or past lives. Professional roles can become blurred and distorted. In analysis, these wishes are analyzed. In music teaching, they are not, although it is my belief that this set of circumstances should be brought to awareness in academia in general and to all music educators and students in particular.

Deeply Disappointed

The date and time of the APsaA program with the performer had been published and were promoted. Members were registering to attend.

A few days before the conference, I received a surprising, gracious, and remorseful email. Our guest explained that there had been an unexpected conflict with his performance schedule about which he had previously been unaware. He was not able to be in New York at the time of the program. He was earnestly apologetic.

Dr. Coen and I felt stunned and disappointed. As we explored our reactions, we also speculated about the performer's feelings. It *was* possible that he did get (or forgot) an invitation to perform elsewhere that conflicted with our conference date. He increasingly was in demand professionally. But we also began to wonder if he started to feel "used" by us for wanting to share his fame. Clearly, it would feel different being interviewed in front of a large audience of psychoanalysts than by a radio host. Might he have had second thoughts about accepting our invitation that subsequently were probed in his own analysis? Perhaps he rethought his quick acceptance that occurred almost a year before the program. We had dismissed our reservations following his acceptance, but had he done the same? Even though he would have received a warm welcome from our audience and hopefully would have enjoyed the spotlight, was he also resentful or at least uncomfortable and beginning to feel we were exploiting him as our "poster boy"? We had not previously been aware of this implication as we consciously acted in good faith. We asked ourselves some hard questions about our possible blindness in the bright aura of a celebrity. Maybe we were assuming too much (or not enough) about our invitation and our excitement that motivated it.

Following this experience, Dr. Coen and I continued to process our reactions as we asked ourselves and each other if we had created a situation that ignited too much discomfort for the celebrity. Did he have an unconscious need or wish to let down a national group of psychoanalysts, possibly as a transference reaction to his own psychoanalyst rooted in mother and father imagoes (i.e., unconscious idealized images)? Was he enacting some aggressive feelings toward his own analyst? Should we have been more attuned to the idea that just because he openly talked about his own psychoanalysis on the radio interview, we were not radio interviewers but an assembly of professional psychoanalysts?[5]

The #MeToo Movement and Music Education

Fame can be seductive.[6] Most of us are not immune to enjoying public praise for our work and accomplishments or being drawn into fame's orbit through an association with well-known people. We all harbor needs, wishes, and hopes which instigate unconscious motivations that both fuel and defend our feelings and behaviors. My wish to better know and collaborate with this celebrity musician is an example of my deeper longings that will be described shortly. Psychoanalyst Salman Akhtar examined the topic of *needs* and *wishes* that focused upon the work of major psychoanalytic theorists.

> Need is universal, wish experience-bound. . . . Although a wish can be replaced by another wish, a need cannot be replaced by another need. Whereas the frustration of a wish causes dynamic shifts, the frustration of a need leads to structural disintegration. Needs and wishes can be in harmony or in opposition.[7]

Akhtar discusses six basic psychological needs.

> (1) the need for one's physical needs to be deemed legitimate; (2) the need for identity, recognition, and affirmation; (3) the need for interpersonal and intrapsychic boundaries; (4) the need for understanding the causes of events; (5) the need for optimal emotional availability of a love object; and (6) the need for a resilient responsiveness by one's love objects under special circumstances. Ordinarily these needs are met during the course of treatment with no deliberate effort by the analyst. In the treatment of some patients, however, they require more direct attention.[8]

In theory and in clinical practice, a distinction between a *need* (biological/instinctual, i.e., destabilizing and permanent) and a *wish* (derivative of a need, i.e., can find substitutes) becomes blurred and extended by other theories. Can we entertain the idea of whether instinctual needs are still the gold standard when thinking about boundary crossings?

Andrea Celenza and Glen Gabbard, psychoanalysts who have studied and treated analysts involved in boundary crossings, suggest positing a role for unmet needs in this process.

> A prominent intrapsychic factor in many cases is unconscious guilt in a male analyst or therapist, usually coinciding with a childhood history of having felt responsible for his mother's unhappiness. Needs for mirroring, affirmation, and recognition may have been neglected early in life. The analyst or therapist [or music performer or teacher] thus presents as a narcissistically vulnerable person who looks primarily or even exclusively to professional activities and relationships for sustenance and affirmation of self-worth.[9] (Brackets mine)

This discussion is relevant to the context of music education as well. Teachers and students, like analysts, have close relationships but inequality in regard to their roles, status, and institutional power. Often there is competition to get accepted into certain music studios (or psychoanalytic institutes or treatment with certain analysts) and then to become the "favorite" student (or patient). It is not unusual to daydream about celebrity-teachers and believe they could magically fulfill our Cinderella wishes and Prince Charming reveries. In those dreams all needs and wishes will be granted, conflicts happily resolved, developmental challenges easily met, and relationships brimming with mutual approval and love ever after. In waking life, teachers, like analysts, cannot fulfill these wishes—and the fantasy that they could do this is a sadomasochistic impediment to the kind of real growth that it is their job to promote.

A "Perfect Storm": Private Music Lessons

While similarities and differences are complex in each analyst-patient or teacher-student dyad, I focus on the music teacher–music student in the remainder of my discussion on boundary crossings. Males contributed to the majority of the studies; female analysts and therapists accounted for 15–20 percent of the cases. Similar dynamics were observed for a "lovesick" female analyst who succumbed to rescue fantasies. I emphasize male music teachers and female students who have been the focus of most research, consulting, and treatment with psychoanalysts (Gabbard and Lester 1995; Gabbard and Peltz 2001; Celenza and Gabbard 2003; Gabbard 2017). I have found the findings and insights of this research about the analytic encounter resonate with me as a metaphor for what can occur between the music teacher and student.

One note on this discussion is important at the outset: *Although boundary-crossing evolves from transference-countertransference enactments by two people,*

sometimes with mutual consent and sometimes without, it is not implied in my
remarks that the victim is responsible for egregious unprofessional behavior.

Studio and private music teachers work with their students in unique
circumstances that can create a potential "perfect storm" requiring both
intimacy and restraint. This storm includes a close music teacher-student
one-to-one relationship (typically lasting over years, as can an analytic
treatment), teaching behind closed doors, physically illustrating technical
approaches on an instrument which can involve touching students to demonstrate challenging musical passages, and using sexually evocative language
and images to shape musical interpretations (e.g., "Make the violin sound
like you are caressing every note"; "Stroke each piano key tenderly to produce a warm sound").

Erotic boundary-crossings need not involve overt sexual activity to
be damaging.[10] For example, declarations of "love," extended time or additional lessons (sometimes scheduled at the teachers' houses), sharing
personal information (particularly about the teachers' private lives), or
commenting on the attractiveness of the students create an erotic atmosphere. These approaches may be rationalized by the teachers as acceptable
pedagogical practice.

Students can become flattered and caught in a web of inappropriate
messages from "lovesick" (Gabbard's label) teachers who justify their blind
impropriety. Such transgressing music teachers often deny or are unaware
of their underlying loss, anger, and hostility that echo their childhood feelings of insufficient nurturing by their mothers early in life. Often aggression
was not identified, discussed, or tolerated in the families, who could appear
to friends and neighbors as ethical and moral individuals. Teaching music
(and being a music student) is at once stimulating, intimate, challenging,
and—at times—frustrating. All these elements combine to arouse transference-countertransference reactions in both students and teachers. Some
teachers project their unexpressed anger onto students who are frustrating
and challenging, which creates "bad" students, reminiscent of the teachers'
inadequate mothers.

Unconsciously, the teachers may be trying to exert control or rescue the
struggling or defiant students whom the teachers also have come to resent.
The teachers cannot tolerate unrelenting challenges that puncture their
perceived omnipotence (e.g., students not responding to pedagogical instruc-
tions, questioning alternative approaches, and generally becoming argumentative and demanding rather than compliant). Some students are severely
depressed and may threaten suicide, looking to the teachers to fix them or
solve their problems. Boundary problems arise when the teachers resort to

their belief that their "love" will rescue the difficult students and themselves by initiating forbidden erotic encounters. The student-teacher relationships can become simultaneously forbidden and exciting.

A Rescue through "Love"

As the teachers "rescue" the students through "love," they also attempt to avoid their aggressive feelings toward the students—feelings that arise in response to what the teachers experience as the students' provocations. However, the teachers' forbidden anger is reaction-formed (i.e., expressed as its opposite), that is, turned into their forbidden "love"—sadistically projected into the very people in displacement (their students) whom they desperately want to love them unconditionally (their mothers). Turned into forbidden, pseudo-loving enactments of the teachers' denied or un-acknowledged anger, the teachers' sexual solution makes the students the objects of their own sadistic projections that can continue to frustrate the teachers. This defensive maneuver that boomerangs perpetuates the teachers' masochistic suffering similar to feelings they experienced from their mothers' emotional unavailability.

Some students are vulnerable to their teachers' "rescue fantasies" to compensate for their own losses and emotional or physical abuses. I am in agreement with Celenza and Gabbard that these relationships are *not* based on mutuality (despite some student-victims' consent). It is not unusual that in trying to understand the perpetrator's motivations, a victim's fragility and oedipal strivings, including aggressive impulses, are not recognized since the teacher's breached professional responsibility is prioritized.

For some teachers who have artistic reputations and who recruit students who are flattered to be invited to join their studios, teaching methods can slide down a slippery slope into boundary violations, sexual or emotional abuse, and psychological pain. The #MeToo movement brought shameful actions that occurred backstage (and behind closed studio doors, in private offices, and in the barricaded unconscious) onto center stage before a national audience. The #MeToo movement has become both a meme and a lightning rod that illustrates how many silenced voices in music and academia increasingly are speaking.

Two important caveats are offered before continuing. First, I emphasize that the majority of teachers, analysts, and professional musicians do *not* violate ethical, social, and psychological norms. They care about students' welfare and personal integrity, and they work appropriately. Second, without an adaptive level of self-importance and narcissism, people would not be able to perform onstage or work as teachers. Healthy narcissism does not impose sadistically upon others. Adaptive narcissism also includes the capacity to recognize and set limits on one's own needs, wishes, and actions informed by a sense of conscience and concern for others' musical and emotional development. Ultimately, it is the responsibility of an idealized teacher as an admired role model to say *no* when inner urges may scream *yes*.

Individuals who are unable to control their sense of importance, omnipotence, entitlement, and grandiosity have the potential to "act out" when feeling deprived or not getting all "the love that ev'ry child oughta get," as sung in *West Side Story* by the Jets to a mocking Officer Krupke, who does not understand his professional role to acknowledge and respond appropriately to their pleas and needs for recognition and help.[11] Some narcissistic teachers believe they can do what they wish with impunity, unable to keep their wishes internalized and sublimated. Some do not recognize the impropriety of their actions when their superegos fail them. Some esteemed faculty proceed from unanalyzed fantasy to unanalyzed action. They have little or no conscious regard for the "other's" bodily or emotional integrity. This is the situation particularly when other people or institutions place the charismatic virtuosos on shiny pedestals and collude and compete with the grandiosity of other competitive institutions for student recruitment as well as for esteemed faculty who tend to bring in revenue.

A Higher Cost for Education

Hostility and feelings of being woefully inadequate are not understood beneath abhorrent actions that are camouflaged as charm, care, and flattery. Such teachers may have been overindulged—or neglected—as young children and harbor anger and hostility "deep down inside them" (as the Jets, repeatedly unheard by Officer Krupke, finally cave into the belief "deep down inside us there's *no good*"). The feeling of needing or being "owed" something often combined with underlying rage for perceived or actual neglect and deprivation becomes projected and enacted with vulnerable "others," typically admiring, impressionable students who do not cause the teacher's sadomasochistic breach of trust. It is not unusual for music students to gravitate to a famous teacher who, perhaps at a summer music camp or music festival, may have promised to help them establish their careers in music. This "promise" is a powerful draw for students in a notably difficult profession, as is offering to help them secure scarce scholarship funds to afford expensive music programs. If some students find themselves in frightening situations they did not anticipate, they may wind up paying a higher price for admission.

Institutional Collusions

Institutions, like individuals, also have narcissistic and grandiose needs as their promotional materials and outreach activities indicate. It is not unusual for institutions to sidestep or avoid curiosity about the perpetrators as well as the individuals who found the courage to report for fear of legal action against the school and possibly administrative blindness and deafness. Secrecy and cover-ups from the top down to hiring committees also motivate silence from other students, faculty, and staff. Victims feel shame and guilt and often bear their trauma silently. Victims may stay quiet also to protect both the teachers and themselves from feared retaliation. The students feel increasingly vulnerable and ultimately trapped. Many music students leave school and abandon their chosen profession altogether. Mental health assessment and treatment needs to be readily and affordably available for all involved.

The Bad Apple Doesn't Fall Far from the Tree

Some organizations confer Golden Apple Awards to professors for "outstanding achievements in the classroom." But what about the "bad apples"? Student abuse by "bad apples" can occur in the context of dysfunctional institutional dynamics. Abuse includes not only sexual activity but also emotional harm that has been described as "soul murder" by Leonard Shengold.[12] There can be a communal "Big Lie" that minimizes or avoids what is occurring behind closed doors and perpetuates a toxic environment for everyone. Some institutions or departments within institutions have a high tolerance for denial and for collusion due to fears of legal action and defer acting on behalf of the victims as well as other students and faculty. The "sound of silence," as in the Simon and Garfunkel classic with its oxymoronic title, is crescendoing from women and men who are raising their voices to report, protest, and promote change.[13]

It is sometimes customary for institutions to dismiss the "bad apples" (a term used by anthropologist and psychoanalyst Muriel Dimen) from teaching duties until legal decisions are resolved.[14] The dismissal of one offending individual does not resolve multiple levels of institutional collusion and dysfunction. It may also attract other unscrupulous people to apply for jobs at institutions that look the other way. Group dynamics of organizations can facilitate the illusion of who is special, demonstrating enchantment with "famous" individuals. These organizations may fear unconsciously that "#TheyToo" may act upon the attributes they ostensibly denounce.

The sound-of-silence norm further implies an unmet plea to examine, reevaluate, and revise the *entire* learning community. As noted by Dimen, "Discourse, or meaning-making, about sexual boundary violations must be open to both thought and feeling, morality and accusation, defense and reflection, personal expression and group expression."[15] How ironic that some music programs that are teaching students how to make sounds with beautiful music have perpetuated silence and nonhealing sounds to address intrapsychic and interpersonal trauma within their own walls.

Treatment Issues

In his thirty-year retrospective study of treating sexual boundary violations of over three hundred psychoanalysts, Gabbard observes that his earlier optimism about preventing future enactments has become more "pessimistic" because rationalizations and pervasive defenses illustrate how some individuals have a different view of ethics when applied toward themselves than toward others. This belief "justifies" their actions since love and hate both exist in the intimate context of therapy and teaching environments. Gabbard emphasizes that loss and grief from earlier developmental experiences are deeper motives experienced by both transgressors and victims so that the analyst or teacher may develop rescue fantasies for saving a distraught patient or student.[16] Gabbard importantly notes that the opportunity for necessary rehabilitation is diminished when appropriate professional help does not exist. As in any treatment, one size does not fit all. The details of each case are unique. While not always the case, single transgressors (i.e., transgressors who maintained multiple violations for weeks or years with the same person) who appeared genuinely regretful and curious about why they acted out may, in general, appear more emotionally available for treatment than multiple transgressors (i.e., transgressors who had multiple violations with different people). I have found in my practice that some individuals, who seek help for fear of being caught, feel so ashamed, humiliated, and anxious that they cannot tolerate engaging deeply with certain topics. For some, it takes several years before they feel safe enough to admit, much less talk about, their transgressions. Instead many have dug into a persistent and argumentative transference with me when we strike a psychological nerve, declaring I do not understand them. At those times, it can feel to me that the patient is inconsolable, like a hurt child speaking to his insensitive mother, and is unreachable because of his agony.

At such times (which often occur after a productive series of sessions), I feel disempowered, incompetent, angry, and tempted to argue back, which alerts me to what is transpiring between us. This allows me to regain some distance from my irritability and to reestablish a mental space where I can think in order to continue the treatment. Over time—typically a great deal of time—the patient may begin to get curious rather than become so hotly defensive when he feels challenged or "caught."

When some violators end illicit relationships, they reassure themselves that they have dealt with their problem so that they do not need further help. Some continue to insist that there was nothing inappropriate about what they did. Saying "sorry" without self-exploration is insufficient to work through other issues that may reveal more severe and ego-dystonic feelings (i.e., those that are inconsistent with one's self-concept). Details by Celenza and Gabbard illustrate how rehabilitation can be lengthy, rigorous, and complex, involve many professionals, and greatly depend on the attitude of the transgressor as much as the enactment that occurred.[17]

Transgressors may be experiencing life crises resembling situations in which any of us could find ourselves. Many are dealing with unrecognized masochism, grandiosity, omnipotence, and narcissistic issues that reflect underlying depression or anxiety. There is the tacit implication that our idealized role models remain pure and untainted by comparison. Most problematic, this denies our own fear of vulnerability by sharply demarcating the type of character who engages in transgressive behavior. We are thus reassured that this cannot happen to us.[18] It is difficult to embrace the idea that under other circumstances, any of us could have impulses without mental guardrails against engaging in abhorrent, destructive behavior. Tempting challenges cannot only be projected onto "them."

Coda

The glitter of celebrity represents unconscious needs that the other person cannot fulfill and that they may use against us, intentionally or not. Because of the power of the unconscious forces at work, it is worth reflecting on how one becomes invested in a powerful celebrity or celebrity-like figure, whether that is a therapist, a music teacher, or an actual superstar. The #MeToo movement has drawn our attention to the need for institutional change. And we must also look within ourselves to understand the dynamics that make the allure of celebrity tempting in the first place.

Dr. Coen and I tried to understand our unconscious motivations that led us to invite a music celebrity to an APsaA conference. We will never know what the performer thought and felt. Since that time and through my personal psychoanalysis and in my own work with patients, my sensitivities about celebrity have both deepened and increased my wish to know a different celebrity.

In reflecting upon my personal interest in illustrious people and reaching out to the performer, I associated to my famous father, a three-time gold-medal winner in speed skating in two Olympic Games. For some reason unknown and unexplained, he left my mother and me when I was four years old. My need and wish to talk with him and learn what happened and why it happened remain alive in my daydreams. These dreams came alive in my personal analysis. In one analytic session, a beloved nursery song spontaneously echoed inside my head. I softly spoke the words to my analyst as my tears welled up.

> Twinkle, twinkle, little star,
> How I wonder what you are!
> Up above the world so high,
> Like a diamond in the sky.
> Twinkle, twinkle, little star,
> How I wonder what you are!

Did my father, the Olympic star, ever wonder about me as I must have wondered what he was like and where he was? Do I combine music and psychoanalysis in my writing with the fantasy of uniting my parents? The mystery of my gold-medal celebrity father will be forever unknown to me.

A radio interview offers anonymity as well as transparency to a speaker. An unseen voice heard by a listener invites fantasy—reminiscent of the analyst seated behind the couch and the patient who does not see the analyst when reclining on the couch. The audience is unseen by a musician playing a concert in a darkened hall. Whatever his reason, the celebrity performer canceled at the last minute and let us down. I realize now that his voice also evoked my longings to get to know my mysteriously absent, celebrity father.

I poignantly and painfully have come to realize that *all that glitters is not gold*.

Notes

1. S. Coen, "The thrall of the negative and how to analyze it," *Journal of the American Psychoanalytic Association* 51 (2003): 465–89.

2. G. O. Gabbard and M. Peltz, "Speaking the Unspeakable: Institutional Reactions to Training Analysts," *J. Amer. Psychoanal. Assn.* 49, no. 2 (2001): 659–67; G. G. Gabbard and E. P. Lester, *Boundaries and Boundary Violations in Psychoanalysis* (New York: Basic Books, 1995); A. Celenza, "Precursors to therapist sexual misconduct: Preliminary findings," *Psychoanal. Psychol.* 15 (1998): 378–97.

3. S. Coen, "Narcissistic Boundary Crossings and How to Manage Them," *Journal of the American Psychoanalytic Association* 55, no. 4 (2007): 1169–90.

4. Gabbard and Lester, *Boundaries*.

5. Not long after this canceled event, Dr. Coen published an article titled "Narcissistic Temptations and Boundary Crossings and How to Manage Them." While he referred to this experience in his article, his focus was on analysts who may become overly involved and overstep boundaries with their impressive patients. I think writing was one way he continued to process what had happened. Now, years later, my own writing allows me to continue to process what happened many years ago.

6. This topic was the focus of a symposium that I chaired at the national meetings of the American Psychoanalytic Association in February 2020 in New York City. In addition to myself as chair and presenter, the panel included Dr. Harriet Wolfe, president of the International Psychoanalytical Association and past president of APsaA (presenting on behalf of Gilbert Kliman, director of the Children's Network); and Dr. Gary Ingle, CEO of the Music Teachers National Association.

7. S. Akhtar, "The Distinction Between Needs and Wishes: Implications for Psychoanalytic Theory and Technique," *Journal of the American Psychoanalytic Association* 47, no. 1 (1999): 113.

8. Akhtar, "The Distinction Between Needs and Wishes," 113. In theory and clinical practice (and writing), a distinction between a *need* (biological/instinctual, i.e., destabilizing and permanent) and a *wish* (derivative of a need, i.e., can find substitutes) becomes blurred and extended with other theories about conflict, deficit, child development, self-psychology, and relational perspectives and more, which leads Akhtar to ask if the ego has moved further away from the id as the original "Gold Standard of need."

9. A. Celenza and G. Gabbard, "Analysts Who Commit Sexual boundary Violations," *Journal of the American Psychoanalytic Association* 51, no. 2 (2003): 623.

10. Gabbard and Peltz, "Speaking the Unspeakable."

11. L. Bernstein et al., "Gee, Officer Krupke," in *West Side Story* (vocal score) (Milwaukee: Leonard Bernstein Music Publishing Company LLC, Boosey and Hawkes, Hal Leonard Corporation, 1957, 1958, 2000).

12. L. M. Shengold, *Soul Murder: The Effects of Childhood Abuse and Deprivation* (New York: Fawcett Columbine, 1989).

13. I am reminded here also of the book *The Rest Is Noise* by Alex Ross (2007), music critic of the *New Yorker*. The title of Ross's book implies that when the music is silent (or there are rests indicated in the score where the music stops), we hear many sounds. As an analyst, I would add that we hear sounds both in the external world (birds, car horns) and in our internal worlds (memories, fantasies, wishes, and needs).

14. M. Dimen, "Eight Topics: A Conversation on Sexual boundary Violations between Charles Amrhein and Murien Dimen," *Psychoanalytic Psychology* 34, no. 2 (2017): 169–74.

15. Dimen, "Eight Topics," 169.

16. G. O. Gabbard, "Sexual Boundary Violations in Psychoanalysis: A 30-Year Retrospective," *Psychoanalytic Psychology* 34, no. 2 (2017): 151–56.

17. Celenza and Gabbard, "Analysts Who Commit."

18. Celenza and Gabbard, "Analysts Who Commit," 620.

CHAPTER EIGHT

~

Rethinking Music Education

The pandemic shone a bright spotlight on the fragility of the music profession. It became painfully and urgently clear how dependent musicians are upon social values, political tastes, and budgets. Music education may or may not address these nonmusical issues, but it is clear in the shadow of COVID-19 that reality and artistry must become better acquainted. We must rethink how we educate musicians just as we rethink what kind of work music can be. Performing music involves *playing* an instrument (which, of course, includes the voice, which is the singer's instrument). However, the *work* of the serious musician is definitely not child's *play*, which, like music, is an important expression of one's intimate self.

Important questions beg for imaginative approaches as we think about how music education can best reach and teach talented, ambitious, and idealistic young people who fall in love with music and subsequently desire to perform it or teach it. Dreams of success and fears of failure have long been part of the fantasies and anxieties of aspiring musicians. The pandemic cruelly thrust musicians into a psychological, social, racial, and economic tsunami with loss of careers and income and many distinctive challenges that persisted during and beyond the 2020 lockdown. It also created new opportunities for opening our eyes to the potential to create new strategies to reinvent and also recreate the heritage of the concert hall and music education that was silenced.

The pandemic darkened concert halls but it did not darken fantasies and dash wishes of those aspiring musicians who found ways to master the internet and use their talent to create innovative programs for audiences, now confined to home and experiencing learning curves on their electronic devices. A new era has begun. Music education always includes much more than playing an instrument or teaching a course. The question now becomes this: How do music educators teach and nurture talented musicians for an unknown future that lies ahead?

Asked and (as Yet) Unanswered Questions

Since children begin music lessons at a very young age, childhood and preadolescent psychological, social, and biological experiences expand our curiosity and attitudes that impact a career choice in music. Does youthful involvement with music suggest different attachments and interactions with parents than other career choices made later in life? For many young people, myself included, early specialization on an instrument and the determination to pursue music as one's life's work can narrow exploration of nonmusic alternatives. Musicians express a "whole" self when playing an instrument. It is not surprising that when the self is under internal or external duress that stage fright surfaces as a shield or defense against deeper, more pervasive fears. While a focus on building technique and repertoire is necessary long before career choice becomes a sharp focus, it can be counterproductive for personality development and vocational investigation if young people do not keep their educational, professional, or social options open or, as I did, go blindly into professional music training immediately after high school. I am not sure if I could have been convinced at that time to do otherwise. Yet one cannot start to become a serious musician until the age of sixteen or eighteen or twenty-five like those aspiring to other careers.

Music educators have an enormous responsibility as students, parents, and teachers ask "How best can we educate talented young people, each of who comes from a unique psychological and cultural background?" Now, more than ever, it is time to learn from the past, incorporate our discoveries meaningfully, and entertain innovative multicultural and interdisciplinary approaches for the future.

Teaching Talented Musicians:
The University and Conservatory

Is it advisable for universities to encourage a focus on specific career goals early in students' undergraduate experience or promote a general curriculum early in young people's college career? Consider the following statement, made over forty years ago, by noted psychologist and educator James Marcia, who developed the Identity Status Interview.

> I think that college curricula should be set up to maximize the occurrence of identity crises and to provide support for their resolution. One current educational practice which would isolate such an attempt is professional training sequences that begin as early as the freshman year. This may be an efficient way of producing engineers and physicians [but is this the same for musicians?], but I suspect that the outcome of this process is more a product than a person. Colleges can become different kinds of places if we begin to look at them in terms of the human life cycle, rather than professional certifiers.[1] (Brackets mine)

How will music programs tune in to the pandemic's multiple lessons? Will there be an emphasis upon graduating efficient "products" or will music programs be more broadly attuned to talented individuals who are in search of how best to devote themselves to establishing a music career? One answer is clear: The process is complex and challenging.

Not only is it important for educators to be aware of the personal, social, and professional dilemmas that musicians face, but also mental health and medical professionals need to appreciate the complicated concerns that bring students to treatment. By understanding career choice in the arts in the context of its centrality to the dynamics of personality development, professionals who treat and teach performers would be able to better interact confidentially with patients and students and offer services and classes that address multidimensional and multicultural complex issues. In fact, music teachers often are the first line of defense to whom students both confide or convey, through various symptoms, that they are in distress. An interdisciplinary approach that combines music, mental, social, economic, and physical issues can lead to psychologically informed educators who teach music students who are not "products but young adults who have been immersed in comprehensive learning and life experiences."[2] Teachers who work with younger students in their private studios have front-row opportunities to be aware of developmental milestones and family involvements. Often the teachers' informed comments and helping students seek professional help when necessary can be life changing. It is important to emphasize here that teachers do not try to be therapists for students any more than therapists try to be music teachers. It is never too early or late to emphasize healthy learning and music-making through collaborations with professionals outside the music profession.

Classes on career options both inside and outside of traditional music careers would be available. Performance anxiety would be studied as a multidetermined symptom with underlying causes. An unbiased review of the literature regarding treatment options would inform students that "one size does not fit all." What does "fit all" is that seeking mental health treatment is not a weakness, a flaw, a stigma, or a sign of lack of talent. It is a strength to seek help to learn music and to learn about oneself when some interference arises. This course could be sensitively and collaboratively taught by a mental health professional and a music teacher. Any professional counseling that is sought by students or teachers would be confidential outside of class. A variety of professionals would be invited guests in classes and could possibly become mentors for students. With video platforms now used widely, this appears to be a possibility rather than relying on travel budgets to bring some guests to campus.

Nurturing Healthy Musicians

Pursuing a career in the performing arts is a lifelong and complex commitment. Musicians begin instrument lessons in early childhood, as (psychologically) the ego and (musically) talent are developing simultaneously. During these vulnerable years and at any age, music teachers and educational protocols can *facilitate or inhibit* creativity, musical and personal growth, and realities about the careers of their students. This may occur when the norm emphasizes or overemphasizes improving technique and winning competitions, stresses the prestige of performance careers (over teaching or other expressions of creativity), denies the psychological implications of playing-related physical injuries, or fails to promote other professional outlets in music or knowledge about possible contributions in professions other than music. Career education in music should emphasize a holistic approach to appreciating one's gifts and how they can be shared with audiences, students, and those people in all walks of life who may never enter a concert hall. Music lessons should be life lessons.

As a way to highlight the ideas I am emphasizing, I refer to a satirical but very serious article written by an esteemed psychoanalyst, Otto Kernberg, MD. His article "Thirty Methods to Destroy the Creativity of Psychoanalytic Candidates" brings important issues into greater focus.[3] Kernberg's provocative "tongue in cheek" slant on psychoanalytic education provides a powerful *positive* statement as it raises awareness about *fostering* creativity and sound mental health in the teaching studio and classroom. Following Kernberg's format, I paraphrase a few ways that music teachers and music schools can *inhibit* the creativity, musical and personal growth, and careers of their students.

How to Destroy Creativity in Music Students:
A Paraphrase of Otto Kernberg

- Do not think of a career in music in the context of the whole person. Insist on better technique, winning competitions, and earning awards to enhance the reputation of the teacher and the school.
- Foster the attitude that self-worth is related to stellar performances and consistently productive practice sessions.
- Deemphasize or ignore the psychological implications of what it means to be injured, ill, or in pain. Do not refer for psychological help for fear of insulting and stigmatizing the student and possibly having him or her leave your class.
- Encourage hierarchies within and between studios and promote favorites among your students to engage in competition with colleagues.
- Discourage students from learning about the numerous professional outlets in music (and other professions) while emphasizing that a performance career is clearly the most prestigious.
- Suggest that teaching is a career chosen by those who cannot succeed in performing careers.
- Convince students that a DMA degree will lead to satisfying work and a high-paying tenured university position.
- Promote the belief that if you are good enough, opportunity will come to you.
- Maintain the attitude that more hours spent practicing will eventually pay off in better performances, public opportunities, and higher earnings. One just has to become "good enough."
- Ignore networking, interpersonal, and valuable communication skills. Courses in such topics take away time from practicing.
- Do not invest in an interdisciplinary career-services program.
- Do not form relationships with professionals in the music and nonmusic community who can be referral resources, guest speakers in classes, or mentors for students.
- Above all, if uncertain about something that may challenge entrenched pedagogical methods, remember that the objective of a music education should be to master, without questioning, established and revered knowledge.

You may chuckle (or shiver) when you read this list, but please reflect seriously upon your reactions and use them as a sounding board to improvise your own thoughts. Do not shy away from any negative reactions that come to your mind since they can evolve into creative solutions.

Educating Healthy People Who Are Musicians

A decision to pursue a career in the performing arts is lifelong and complex. There are many important issues that students, parents, university faculty, private teachers, and administrators working together must consider in assisting musicians to bring their hard work and dreams to fulfillment or satisfying redirection.

With these complexities in mind over many years, I have supported the following:

- Psychological and physical interdisciplinary programs and courses in the curriculum would be established that are equal in importance to private lessons, music theory, music history, and academic courses.
- Interdisciplinary courses would include study in the psychology of stage fright from multiple perspectives, physiology of the performer, professional networking, audition strategies, career management (i.e., interviewing, résumé writing, finances), nutrition, and exercise.
- The courses would be taught by invited interdisciplinary faculty and guests and emphasize multicultural music-making.
- An active career center for music students and alumni would be established.
- Data on graduates would be collected routinely by the university, who would follow the careers of alumni.
- Outreach courses would find opportunities for student performances (including lectures, recitals, and residencies in communities and schools) to provide greater involvement speaking about and performing music in the local and national community, public and private schools, underserved and minority locations, social events, assisted-living facilities, home gatherings, and anywhere music can be included creatively.
- Students would be coached on how to become visible, audible, and heard musically in political, social, and multicultural settings.
- Relationships would be forged with agents and publicists to assist graduates of music programs in finding employment. Public-relations and marketing or financial experts would be invited to interact with students.
- The message would emphasize that YOU are your own best advocate for the importance of music in a performer's life as well as the value of music in the lives of others.
- Professional psychological help, without stigma, would be encouraged when personal issues interfere.

- Teachers and administrators would benefit from becoming increasingly sensitized to the enormous impact of their relationships both with their colleagues and with their students.
- There would be a resource center where teachers could confidentially discuss teaching concerns and obtain referrals for psychological treatment.
- Legal advice and psychological assistance would be available to all students, faculty, and staff to report and discuss uncomfortable interactions. This resource would emphasize privacy and safety and would destigmatize the label of reporting what has been experienced as inappropriate.
- Faculty would be encouraged to recognize their own psychological and professional vulnerabilities and strengths. Confidential professional resources and consultants would be available for them.

It is important for teachers to tune into the dynamics of psychological, social, and emotional development as well as the dynamics in the musical scores to hear what students both say and play. Whether one remains in a career in music, combines music with another discipline, or leaves the profession altogether, the process is a long excursion with many possible crossroads, bumps, detours, and pleasures. By the time a serious career in music is pursued, many emotional factors have coalesced in ways that can be helpful or unhelpful and can become confusing at times. In the process, the teacher becomes a central figure representing both a parent-substitute and a professional role model. Early interactions with family, peers, and society who have formed the original building blocks of intrapsychic and interpersonal relationships become projected upon teachers and audiences, who have the perceived and real capacity to love or leave you. Thus, the vulnerability of the young child who begins an instrument and travels a path toward professional training cannot be overstated.

It has felt imperative to me for years, not optional, that the establishment of psychological and interdisciplinary programs in the curriculum is a relevant and important aspect of healthy music-making that is as important as music theory and history and offering career services to assist students with concrete issues in both performance and nonperformance careers.[4] Support for the "whole person" throughout life is a birthright, not an option. It is the responsibility of those who nurture and educate musicians from their earliest lessons through their professional aspirations and preparations to teach musicians how to nurture themselves.

A Healthy Music Profession

Both teachers and therapists need to recognize the importance of their strengths, limits, assets, and boundaries. A therapist (even a musically trained one) should no more try to teach music to a patient in a session than a psychologically sensitive teacher should engage in therapy with a student in a lesson. Referral networks must be established and utilized for consultations for faculty, administrators, and students. Recognizing when and knowing how to refer for professional counseling, therapy, and consultations with mental health or medical professionals when appropriate is important. While I am not advocating that every student or teacher should consult a therapist or physician, at times both the teacher and student could benefit from confidential professional support. In particular, the negative stigma of seeking psychological help needs to be addressed candidly and replaced with the positive attitude that dealing with mental health is a strength that promotes self-care. Formal research and funding about the specialized psychological and medical needs of musicians and music curricula are also important aspects of healthy music programs.

Inroads toward these significant goals (pedagogical, clinical, and research) have been made by a number of music, psychological, and psychoanalytic programs. Increased establishment of innovative interdisciplinary focus about the relationship among the arts, artists, mental health, and society is both a short- and long-term goal. Such efforts repeatedly emphasize the importance of a curriculum dedicated to training healthy musicians—or what I prefer to think of as teaching *healthy people* who are musicians.

Teaching an instrument is so much more than teaching to play the "right notes" or perform brilliantly and sensitively. While psychological hardiness and technical dexterity are necessary to navigate the challenges of the music profession, psychic income from the immeasurable gratification of playing virtuosically and perceptively does not pay bills, buy love, or feed egos for very long. Sometimes, perhaps too often in the music profession, the ego suffers, psychological pain or physical illness occurs, and career plans are altered or derailed altogether. It is harrowing to entertain the idea that music education trains people for unemployment, underemployment, anxiety, and depression. A healthy music profession will prepare its future emissaries to deal creatively and adaptively with unique personal challenges and cultural opportunities as career choices.

Congratulations are in order to those individuals and teachers who have tried to develop ongoing *in-depth* interdisciplinary programs in their private studios and at their schools and universities. Why hasn't every music school explored and moved this topic to the top of its agenda? While no one disagrees, in principle, with the ideas I have offered, challenges occur at many universities and colleges, on many levels, to formally institute in-depth, required, comprehensive health-related programs into the music curriculum.

I have often heard, "We would like to have mental health programs for our students but we do not have the money to afford what it would take." A frequent reason voiced points to the "budget." Dollars and cents are always real concerns, although I believe grants could be obtained for promoting health in music education. There is much more to the "cost question" (as we have seen in the discussion about the meaning of money in chapter 4). There is a higher price to be paid for shortchanging the psychological and physical health of music students with programs that do not optimize their well-being, professional identity, and contribution to the arts and to society.

The ego and talent develop simultaneously over a lifetime. One's identity becomes enmeshed in playing an instrument. The fear of losing it "all" through probing issues other than learning notes, theory, and other music topics can inhibit personal development and professional growth. Such fears run deep in students, teachers, and administrators who may feel uncomfortable about opening themselves and the curriculum up for scrutiny. This discomfort may be embedded in "rational" answers about budgets which can hide misinformed and unfortunate stigmas about mental health that delays or prevents reevaluation and creative innovation.

Clinical experience and research findings regarding creativity, productivity, and performance inhibitions put these notions to rest. Knowledge about oneself and about what fosters or inhibits professional growth is empowering. It is time now for private music instructors and all music schools and universities to prioritize and demand the necessary resources to invest in the health of their most valuable assets, their students, all of who have the potential to become psychologically healthy cultural ambassadors of the present and in the future.

Notes

1. J. D. Marcia, "Studies in Ego Identity" (unpublished research, Simon Fraser University, 1976).

2. J. J. Nagel, *Managing Stage Fright* (New York: Oxford University Press, 2017).

3. O. Kernberg, "Thirty Methods to Destroy the Creativity of Psychoanalytic Candidates," *Int. Journal Psychoanalysis* 77 (1996): 1031–40. "Candidate" is the term for MDs, PhDs, and MSWs who undergo intensive clinical training for many years of additional in-depth work in mental health treatment after earning their professional degrees and already have entered clinical practice as fully licensed professionals.

4. J. J. Nagel, "How to Destroy Creativity in Music Students: The Need for Emotional and Psychological Support Services in Music Schools," *Medical Problems of Performing Artists* 24 (2009): 15–17.

CHAPTER NINE

⁓

Music and Mind Outside the Box

Due to the pandemic with its dark and empty concert halls and canceled music classes and lessons, musicians of all ages have been forced to think outside their traditional music box. The warmth and energy shared between people attending and giving live performances and interacting in teaching studios, at one time safe places for music communication, mentorship, and social and cultural interaction, has been difficult or absent during the persistence of the unrelenting pandemic. This sudden change in musical culture has upended musicians' lives, incomes, and emotions.

Anthony Tommasini, retired chief music critic for the *New York Times*, recently was appointed to teach a course on critical listening at Juilliard, exemplifying the transitions musicians can and do make even when classical music is undergoing seismic changes. In his final column, he wrote, "I've been continually impressed by the entrepreneurial energy of artists—who realizing that traditional career paths were becoming limited, and that major institutions were overlooking new generations of creators—ventured off on their own . . . to create their own groups and put on concerts anywhere, anyhow."[1] After catching their breath following the cataclysmic shock of decimated career plans and aspirations, numerous musicians have been doing exactly this.

In the coming years, careers in music will require innovation. Many years of unquestioned but presently reexamined routines offer new possibilities for creative growth. An openness to all kinds of artistic expression and novel thoughts, activities, and gratifications await the musician who defies the status quo. I remain deeply optimistic about the enduring value of music and the contributions of those people who choose careers in music, or, more likely, who were chosen by music.

The Value of Music: Past and Future

Why is music valuable in our mental and social lives? Many people enjoy music, i.e., listening to it, teaching it, and playing it and even coping with stage fright to perform it. But really, why should anyone care about music? Scholars throughout history have tried to crack the "code" of why and how music affects us so deeply.[2]

In the fantasy drama piece A Conversation between Mozart and Freud, the composer challenges the psychoanalyst's disdain for music when Freud explains that "with music, I am almost incapable of obtaining any pleasure."[3] Freud maintains he cannot appreciate something he does not understand. Mozart counters Freud and suggests that in addition to Freud's discovery that dreams are the Royal Oral—*verbal*—Road to the unconscious, music travels a parallel path on a Royal Aural—*nonverbal*—Road to the same destination. As such, music evokes powerful emotions, awakens memories, and allows new creative ideas to surface in the dreamer—without the dreamer trying to generate those ideas consciously. Their conversation proceeds to explore many aspects of the importance of music and words in mental life as they also begin to revisit Mozart's groundbreaking *Piano Sonata K. 310 in A Minor*, written the summer the composer's mother died when traveling with him. Mozart's grief is expressed through his music and his change in compositional style that suggests he was beginning to compose beyond traditional classical boundaries.[4] The two icons return to Eternity without ever resolving their differences and leave us pondering not only the questions they raised but also how musicians in our own time of loss and grief will move beyond established traditional conventions in their music careers.

Psychoanalytic and musical principles together and separately, as discussed by Mozart and Freud, can provide expanded creative insights and emotional healing inside and outside the consulting room and concert hall. There can be pleasure, intimacy, and insight gained from interacting with patients, audiences, and performers and from offering presentations in places that make both musicians and mental health professionals stretch their concepts of career and work. These concepts include new versions of work space, and our long-accepted (often unquestioned) sense of "tradition" as we are contemporary "Mozarts and Freuds." Musicians already have shown the initiative to venture into creative, challenging, and imaginative work environments.

Music serves innumerable purposes in our lives. Music is played at weddings and funerals and is subliminally piped into grocery stores and shopping malls to encourage purchasing as well as at the dentist's office to reduce anxiety. The use of earbuds, which have become as stylish as earrings, comes as close to having music in your head as you can without having music artificially implanted or naturally generated inside your brain. Even Mother Nature serenades us with birdcalls, wind gusts, horn beeps, children's play, babies' cries, and siren screams. Each of us would hear a different rendering of a composition by John Cage titled *4'33"* (Four Minutes and Thirty-Three Seconds), in which a performer or orchestra (or any instrumental combination) sits silently.[5] Audiences are left with their own reactions about sounds that penetrate their aural and emotional spaces.[6]

I vividly remember listening alone to a recording of the "Masque" movement in *The Age of Anxiety* (Symphony no. 2) by Leonard Bernstein as it comforted me following the untimely death of my mother when I was a student at Juilliard. The music reassured me in ways that words could not at that time. How ironic during COVID-19 that a masque/mask shut out a life-threatening virus as our emotional lives were also metaphorically shut out and masked from the joys of in-person relationships and sharing music with others in public settings.

Music can be an integral part of our emotional cushion for trauma throughout life and most currently from COVID-19. Music also heightens joy in times of celebration. The formal qualities of Western music (i.e., pitch, rhythm, dynamics, melody, tempo, and formal structure) enable us to expect certain compositional techniques that bring predictability to our ears. Music from other traditions can offer similar benefits, which ideally will be increasingly clear in creative collaborations between different social groups and cultures. As an analyst, I listen to the tone of voice and nuance in my patients' associations, the rhythms of their speech, and the timing and length of their silences, an aural clinical technique that is comparable to the careful listening acquired as a musician.

The Impact of Music: Historical Precedents

There are historical precedents that music and musicians have influenced social policy, cultural trends, and education reform. Music has been used to energize and suppress political movements and dictate compositional styles. Indeed, musicians can be politicians, diplomats, and cultural ambassadors in the world arena, in their communities, and at institutions. Mozart belonged to the Illuminati branch of the Freemasons and used musical motives in his compositions (to connote symbolically the Masonic ideals of courage and resilience). A candidate seeking entrance into the Freemasons would knock three times to gain entrance to the initiation ceremony. This musical metaphor is expressed in the three repeated chords in the overture in *The Magic Flute*.

Giuseppe Verdi tirelessly advocated for nationalism (Risorgimento) and the unification of Italy. His operas were musical testaments to his political and social beliefs. Verdi advocated for the repeal of the government's box-office tax, paying appropriate orchestral salaries, supporting music education for students, and promoting subsidies for the arts in Naples, Italy. He became a member of the Italian Parliament and an appointed member of the Senate. At his funeral, a large Italian crowd sang the popular chorus of the Hebrew slaves (*"Va, Pensiero"*) from his opera *Nabucco*, which celebrated the longings for the promised land by the Hebrews. Italians were aware of the double meaning in this song and Verdi's call for unification in Italy. Alex Ross wrote in the *New Yorker*, "In the past century and a half, the quiet majesty of 'Va, pensiero' has spoken many times in periods of crisis, and its usefulness is not at an end. In the modern world, we seldom find ourselves in the grip of a single emotion, and this is what Verdi restores to us—the sense of belonging."[7]

I have posed this question about the power of music in another publication.[8] What it is about music that resonates inside of us when words fall short is an eternal mystery at least objectively. We can experience feelings listening to music that have not yet found words.[9] Emotions out of sight are not out of mind. Words often feel inadequate because they are. You can close your eyes and cover your face, but you cannot purposefully turn off your hearing and mask the melodies in your mind.

In 1957, Leonard Bernstein's music in *West Side Story* made its debut sonically illustrating racial and psychological tensions between and within the Caucasian Jets and the Puerto Rican Sharks. The conflicts expressed in music and between the gangs reflect and evoke tensions and the love and hate that also exist inside our minds. Music can evoke strong feelings in us that we hear in the characters onstage. A lifelong champion of peace, Bernstein delivered a speech at his alma mater, Harvard, in 1986 during a time of international terrorism. Pan Am flight 73 had been hijacked and bombings erupted in Paris. Threats had recently accompanied Bernstein's tour with the Israel Philharmonic in Vienna after Kurt Waldheim, former Nazi intelligence officer, was elected president of Austria. Bernstein emphasized, "The stronger the defense, the greater the threat must be. . . . I suddenly realized that this is the way the world lives . . . existing in terms of an enemy."[10]

The "enemy" is both externally and internally represented inside our minds and reveals social, political, cultural, and psychological issues embedded in racism, oppression, and prejudice.

Musicians and Mental Health Professionals as Nontraditional First Responders

The function of music and musicians continues to be invented. Musicians were among the most immediately and adversely affected victims of the loss of both real dollars and psychic income during COVID-19. With all performances abruptly canceled, schools placed on lockdown, and music lessons interrupted, many musicians had to hustle to find work of any kind to pay for their basic needs. It was anticipated that vaccines, boosters, and masks would allow us to return to normal, or more likely to establish a "new normal." With unexpected COVID variants, this has not been the case (as of this writing). The pandemic continues to survive in our masked, vaccinated, and boosted midst. The psychological effects of COVID-19 will linger emotionally long after science has tempered its most severe dangers. Musicians are on the cultural and social front lines to provide comfort to help mitigate some of the trauma inflicted by COVID-19's relentless cruelty.

During the pandemic, many recitals, private lessons, master classes, concerts, and music classes taught in schools have benefited from technology which allowed a wide audience to experience music performances from their homes. It became clear that this audience was more diverse than those who typically could afford to attend formal concerts or go to school safely. The same was true for psychotherapists and psychoanalysts and their patients who adjusted to the learning curve of teletherapy. Music and musicians reached out beyond the boundaries of the traditional teaching studio and concert hall. Opportunity to share music was discovered in the ashes of the COVID-19 disaster in nontraditional venues, including living rooms, nursing homes, businesses, driveways, garages, lawns, and other creative stages. Musicians and audiences began to interact virtually.

Music and Therapy in and beyond the Consulting Room

The healing power of music has been apparent to me personally and in my work for a long time. During the past two-plus years of COVID-19, I have heard my colleagues speak spontaneously about music's impact on their moods. Dr. T found it soothing to listen to a particular composition when he mourned the death of his father. One colleague and I exchanged emails that always contained YouTube music videos. I have attended professional meetings on Zoom where music was played to conclude the sessions. My patient Ms. B was humming as she entered her Zoom session with me. She told me that she had attended a concert on the internet and wished I could have shared it. I noted that she *was* sharing her musical experience with me and wondered if she had more to say. Indeed she did! Music often is heard inside our minds inside and outside the consulting room and music venues when we listen for it in ourselves and also hear it in others.

Some of my patients burst into song about celebrations, life-cycle events, and losses as music evokes happy and sad memories. I cannot forget a group of children with whom I worked some years ago who could not speak but could comprehend what was said to them. The students had individualized computers adapted to their levels of skill on which they could express themselves. I used music to communicate with them. One child cried as he told me, through his special device, about his parents' divorce. An adolescent girl shared her excitement about wearing eye shadow. Together we were able to communicate via music in a way that allowed the students to share feelings otherwise silenced inside them.

Music and mind can come together in unexpected ways and at unexpected places. Following the devastation of Hurricane Katrina in 2005, I was invited to give a presentation at the New Orleans-Birmingham Psychoanalytic Center. After many months, the opera house was reopening with Donizetti's opera *Lucia di Lammermoor*. At the intermission of the opera, the woman sitting next to me in the audience started to tell me, a stranger, how she had lost her home and that her family who lived near her for years recently was forced to move out of state to find employment. She was so sad and commented that she had been deeply moved by the opera. She did not know I was a therapist or a musician, but she quickly realized I had an ear willing to listen, to share the power of Donizetti's music, and to mourn her losses with her as she poured out her story. I never learned her name but I have never forgotten her or that intermission.

When people feel understood, they become open to new ways to think about long-standing issues and begin to realize that the flawlessness they seek from themselves and others can benefit from mental modifications to better appreciate their competence instead of self-defeating searches for perfection. Some individuals burn out, become cynical, and sometimes give up altogether when they cannot achieve their wished-for goals. Fresh insights, often gained through music, exploration of feelings, and a belief that others care about them (such as teachers, therapists, mentors, and even strangers—

all evoking early relationships with parents), can permit old perspectives to become the basis for fresh change.

Beyond the Teaching Studio and Concert Hall

The pandemic has brought creative opportunities and challenges for musicians who are willing to be emotionally open to using their traditional training in music in nontraditional settings. Musicians also will benefit from learning music from people unlike themselves to interact with individuals from different cultures and backgrounds. Musicians are on the cultural and social front lines to provide comfort and caring to help mitigate some of the trauma inflicted by COVID-19's relentless, cruel stubbornness. Options for musicians post-pandemic are gradually emerging that can evolve into creative new career directions. Perhaps it took the pandemic to viscerally convince us that we must reach out further and more personally to others more than previously imagined.

Career choices in music beyond the pandemic involve more than teaching and performing. More than ever, career choices are open to innovation and communication. The power of music and the arts can address poverty, crime, gun safety, public health, racism, gender discrimination, and mental health crises when emphasizing the lasting values that music and compassionate understanding for others bring to our lives.

The role of a well-rounded music-citizen, from earliest lessons through professional training and beyond, illustrates how interdisciplinary efforts to educate musicians on instruments include knowledge about our own humanity as musicians who care about others with a broader view of social and cultural issues. Those individuals who teach and make music are on the front lines to bring pleasure, have an effect on emotional healing, and address global, national, and local priorities. In other words, music education can emphasize more than creating teachers and performing virtuosos. Music can and must bring a powerful message to the public, to lawmakers, and to funding sources that music is vital to the soul of our nation.

Thinking from a humanitarian and global perspective, music teachers are placed in a significant and responsible position to nurture students who, in turn, can nurture and educate the general public and public officials about the value of the arts in society, indeed in the world. Institutions and teachers who educate musicians are responsible, post-pandemic more than ever, for graduating cultural ambassadors. Music students should demand nothing less from their education.

A change in music education will require both a change in attitudes of the leaders in the profession and also a change in those people who decide to pursue music careers to commit themselves to an expanded role in society. It takes a village of professionals who can collaborate with new vision and a redesigned version of career to bring music to a recovering post-pandemic public in a music-starved society.

Teachers and performers also need to become tuned into the personal toll the pandemic has taken on their occupation and their emotional lives. Caring about others also involves self-care. Personal disappointments and career burnout, physical issues, emotional struggles, and economic concerns about future work are but a few of the urgencies that need attention at all times and particularly in the aftermath of interrupted dreams, personal needs, and career losses. Unattended (which includes not seeking professional help when needed or having that assistance readily available to musicians), these issues can have long-haul consequences both mentally and physically.

Has Anything Good Resulted from the Pandemic?

Now, better armed with vaccines, masks, and some expertise with technology, we reflect upon the difficulties and the opportunities that this human tragedy has brought, unasked, to our previously unmasked lives.[11] If anything good professionally has come from the pandemic for me, working clinically and through applied and interdisciplinary writing and collaborations with musicians has deepened my strong convictions about the power of music in our lives.

Psychoanalyst Isaac Tylim maintained, "9-11 brought analysis onto the streets and piers."[12] Has the pandemic brought musicians into the streets and other creative venues? In his visionary book published in 2005, *The Artist as Citizen*, Joseph Polisi crystallizes what had been clear all along pre-pandemic. To paraphrase Polisi:

> Music (*psychoanalytic*) education involves more than teaching performers (*psychoanalysts*) but also nurtures innovators and communicators. A change in music (*psychoanalytic*) education will require a change in attitudes of the leaders in the profession, particularly music (*psychoanalytic*) educators and administrators who commit to training educated performers (*psychoanalysts*) attuned to their role in society.[13] (Parentheses are my additions)

As we talk about "otherness," it feels inevitable that we can demonstrate our willingness to participate in work that is musically "other" from what we pursued pre-pandemic. Now more than ever, music and psychoanalysis rely on our ingenuity, boldness, and resourcefulness to promote their enduring and endearing value. An expanded vision to blend music and psychoanalysis, for me, can offer a verbal and sonic antibody for our traumatized country and battered psyches. Musicians can create multiple creative programs in the larger community coping with cultural, social, public-health, racial, environmental, economic, medical, and mental maladies.

When we strive to be *a part of* rather than *apart from* playing an expanded role in society, we introduce controversies and intricacies into our existing theories, educational training, and practice which can challenge our physical and psychic comfort zones. As we listen to the musical nuances inherent in words and find words to verbalize the untapped music and feelings deep within ourselves and others, we discover new creative possibilities. If the pandemic has taught me anything, it is that the time for reaching both inside and outside our theories and beyond our comfort zones is overdue. It is now.

A Conclusion and a Beginning

The pandemic has compelled us to pause at a crossroad and look backward to learn from history, forward to imagine society championing the intrinsic value of the arts, inward to reflect upon our own feelings and life experiences, and to the future to establish effective music and mental health programs through interdisciplinary collaborations. Musicians can become cultural ambassadors when working with others to share the intrinsic value of music as essential for mental, physical, and social and public health.

Despite its harsh and cruel lessons, the pandemic has taught us that the internal flame that fuels career choice in music may flicker or dim, but, unextinguished, it also rises to ignite fresh challenges and rewards beyond the pandemic. Indeed, career choices in music *are* some of the most significant decisions we make in our lifetime.

Notes

1. A. Tommasini, "What Shouldn't Change about Classical Music," *New York Times*, November 17, 2022.

2. S. K. Langer, *Philosophy in a New Key: A Study in the Symbolism of Reason, Rite, and Art* (Cambridge: Harvard University Press, 1942, 1957); H. Kohut and S. Levarie, "On the Enjoyment of Listening to Music," *Psychoanalytic Quarterly* 19 (1950): 64–87; C. Lipson, "The Meanings and Functions of Tunes That Come into One's Head," *Psychoanalytic Quarterly* 75, no. 3 (2006): 859–78; P. Noy, "The

Psychodynamics of Music," *Journal of Music Therapy* 3(4): 126–34, 4(1): 7–23, 4(2): 45–51, 4(3): 81–94, 4(4): 117–25, 1966–1967; S. Feder, "'Promissory Notes': Method in Music and Applied Psychoanalysis," in *Psychoanalytic Explorations in Music*, eds. S. Feder, R. L. Karmel, and G. J. Pollock (Madison: International Universities Press, 1993), 3–19; J. J. Nagel, *Melodies of the Mind* (London: Routledge, 2013).

3. J. J. Nagel, "Music, Chapter 32, A Conversation between Mozart and Freud," in *Textbook of Applied Psychoanalysis*, eds. S. Akhtar and S. Twemlow (London: Routledge/Taylor and Francis, 2018); Freud, *On narcissism*, 211. This conversation was performed at Steinway Hall in New York City February 13, 2020.

4. It is unclear if Mozart composed his *Piano Sonata K. 310* before or after his mother's death on July 3, 1778, but it is clear it was written during a period of turmoil for the composer in "summer 1778" and departed from his accustomed compositional style. Further, he wrote to his father six days after his mother passed away that "this was the saddest day of my life." Emily Anderson, *The Letters of Mozart and His Family*, 1938, completed in 1966 by A. Hyatt King and Monica Carolan (London: Macmillan; New York: St. Martin's Press, 1966), 561.

5. W. Hermes, "The Story of '4'33,'" The NPR100, 2000, https://www.npr.org/2000/05/08/1073885/4-33.

6. This composition can be performed by a soloist or any combination of instruments. Alex Ross, music critic for the *New Yorker*, has emphasized this idea in his 2007 book *The Rest Is Noise*.

7. Alex Ross, "Verdi's Grip," *The New Yorker*, September 24, 2001, 32–35, https://www.newyorker.com/magazine/2001/09/24/verdis-grip.

8. Nagel, *Melodies*.

9. Nagel, *Melodies*. Music is used as "data" to address the question "What is it about music that resonates inside listeners when words fall short?"

10. C. Oja and M. Horowitz, "Introduction: Something Called Terrorism," speech given at Harvard University, fall 1986, by Leonard Bernstein, *The American Scholar* (2008): 71–79.

11. J. J. Nagel, "Beyond the Consulting Room: How I Discovered 'Heard' Immunity Through Music and Psychoanalytic Knowledge," *The American Psychoanalyst* (fall 2022): 23–24.

12. I. Tylim, "Becoming a Psychoanalyst in the Age of Diminishing Expectations: Psychoanalysis in the United Nations," *International Journal of Applied Psychoanalytic Studies* 6, no. 1 (2009): 94–9.

13. J. Polisi, *The Artist as Citizen* (New York: Amadeus Press, 2005), 11.

Select Bibliography

Arcocella, Joan. "What Went Wrong at New York City Ballet." *New Yorker*, February 11, 2019. https://www.newyorker.com/magazine/2019/02/18/what-went-wrong -at-new-york-city-ballet.

Bernstein, Leonard. *The Joy of Music*. New York: Simon and Schuster, 1954.

Kantor, Jodi, and Meghan Twohey. *She Said: Breaking the Sexual Harassment Story that Helped Ignite a Movement*. New York: Penguin Press, 2019.

Nagel, Julie J. Blog of Dr. Julie Jaffee Nagel. https://julienagel.net.

Nagel, Julie J. *Managing Stage Fright: A Guide for Musicians and Music Teachers*. New York: Oxford University Press, 2017.

Nagel, Julie J. *Melodies of the Mind: Connections Between Psychoanalysis and Music*. East Sussex: Routledge, 2013.

National Endowment for the Arts. www.arts.gov.

National Endowment for the Arts. *The Art of Reopening: A Guide to Current Practices among Arts Organizations During COVID-19*. Washington, D.C.: National Endowment for the Arts, 2021. https://www.arts.gov/sites/default/files/The%20 Art-of-Reopening.pdf.

Parker, Kim, Juliana M. Horowitz, and Rachel Minkin. "How the Coronavirus Outbreak Has—and Hasn't—Changed the Way Americans Work." Pew Research Center, December 9, 2020. https://www.pewresearch.org/social-trends/2020/12/09 /how-the-coronavirus-outbreak-has-and-hasnt-changed-the-way-americans-work/.

Polisi, Joseph W. *Beacon to the World: A History of Lincoln Center*. New Haven: Yale University Press, 2022.

Popova, Maria. "Leonard Cohen on Creativity, Hard Work, and Why You Should Never Quit before You Know What It Is You're Quitting." *The Marginalian*, July 15, 2014. https://www.themarginalian.org/2014/07/15/leonard-cohen-paul-zollo -creativity/.

Ross, Alex. "Davóne Tines Is Changing What It Means to Be a Classical Singer." *New Yorker*, November 15, 2021. https://www.newyorker.com/magazine/2021/11/22 /davone-tines-is-changing-what-it-means-to-be-a-classical-singer.

Ross, Alex. *Listen to This*. New York: Farrar, Straus and Giroux, 2010.

Steinhardt, Arnold. "A Musician's Curse." The Key of Strawberry blog. https://keyof strawberry.com/a-musicians-curse/.

Steinhardt, Arnold. *Violin Dreams*. Boston: Houghton Mifflin Company, 2006.

Terkel, Studs. *Working: People Talk about What They Do All Day and How They Feel about What They Do*. New York: The New Press, 1972.

Verrett, Shirley. *I Never Walked Alone: The Autobiography of an American Singer*. Hoboken: John Wiley & Sons, Inc., 2003.

Index

113

of magic thinking, 74–75
Lucia di Lammermoor (Donizetti), 106
lullaby, as transitional object, 33

The Magic Flute (Mozart, W. A.), 104
magic thinking, 47n11;
  in childhood, 26, 34;
  competence and, 70;
  loss of, 74–75;
  perfection in, 67
Marcia, James, xv, 60, 93
Maslow, Abraham, 24–25, 46n3
mass media, performance and, 13
McDonald, Marjorie, 33
mental health, 18;
  advocacy for, xvi–xvii;
  first responder role in, 105;
  in music education, 94
#MeToo movement, 99;
  abuse in music education and,
    81–86;
  celebrity and, xvi, 84–85;
  institutional change and, 88;
  psychoanalysts and, 87–88;
  silences and, 84
Michigan, Ann Arbor, 34
Michigan Psychoanalytic Institute,
    University of Michigan, xii, 3
mistrust *versus* trust, 30–32
money, 8, 10–11, 20–21;
  choice between music and, 19;
  musician as product worth, 12–13,
    54;
  nonmusic jobs providing, 2, 9, 14,
    49, 53;
  psychic income and, 50–51, 54–57;
  stage fright and, 52–54;
  uncertainty and, 7, 15–19
motives, in career choice, xiii, xiv, 2, 4
Mozart, Leopold, 57n6
Mozart, Wolfgang Amadeus, 23, 55;
  Freemasons and, 103–4;
  The Magic Flute, 104;

Piano Sonata K. 310 in A Minor of,
    102, 110n4
Mr. D (patient), 73–74
Ms. B (patient), 106
Ms. G (patient), 72–73
music, as data, 110n9
Music Disaster Relief Grant, Austin,
    Texas, 21n12
musicians, xv, 11–12, 27, 91, 102;
  arts funding and, 10, 14;
  creativity and, 5;
  economic knowledge of, 56;
  entrepreneurialism of, 14;
  Erikson's Eight Stages for, 29–47;
  income gap for, 10, 13;
  patronage of, 55;
  as product worth money, 13, 54;
  role in society of, xiii, xiv, xvi, 4, 19,
    96, 99, 107, 109;
  value of, 2, 8, 17, 102–5
music lessons, private, risk of boundary
    crossing in, 82–85
Music Teachers National Association,
    90n6

Nabucco (Verdi), 104
narcissism, healthy, 84–85
National Endowment for the Arts
    (NEA), xiv–xv, 10–11, 16, 19n1,
    20n8, 21n13;
  employment and wage data from, 10,
    20n3
National Music Camp, Interlochen,
    Michigan, xii
National Public Radio (NPR), 77–78
NEA. *See* National Endowment for the
    Arts
needs:
  Maslow on, 24–25;
  self-worth and basic, 50;
  six basic psychological, 81;
  wishes as compared to, 81, 90n8
neglect, in infancy, 30–31

~

About the Author

Julie Jaffee Nagel, PhD, is a psychologist, psychoanalyst, and musician who brings her unique combination of experience and education in music and mental health to a nuanced understanding of her clinical and interdisciplinary work. She is a graduate of the Juilliard School (BM and MS, piano), the University of Michigan (MSW, MA, PhD, psychology and social work), and the Michigan Psychoanalytic Institute (adult psychoanalysis).

She has given presentations and seminars locally, nationally, and internationally including "Stage Fright," "Careers in the Arts," "#MeToo and Music Education," "The Value of Music in Mental Life," and "Injustice, Oppression, and Prejudice as 'Heard' in Music." Her fantasy dialogue *A Conversation between Mozart and Freud* was performed in Steinway Hall in New York City in February 2020 (just before the COVID-19 lockdown). She is the author of *Managing Stage Fright: A Guide for Musicians and Music Teachers* (Oxford University Press, 2017) and *Melodies of the Mind* (Routledge, 2013) and has published numerous articles in major peer-reviewed psychoanalytic journals and music publications.

She has been active for many years in the American Psychoanalytic Association, where she was chair of the program Psychoanalytic Perspectives on Music, and in the College Music Society, the Music Teachers National Association, and the National Conference on Keyboard Pedagogy, from whom she received their distinguished service award. Additional awards include two Nathan Segel Awards (Michigan Psychoanalytic Institute), the Karl Menninger Award, and the Ernst and Gertrude Ticho Award (American Psychoanalytic Association) for contributions in both psychoanalysis and music.

Her latest book, *Career Choices in Music beyond the Pandemic: Musical and Psychological Perspectives* (Rowman and Littlefield, 2023), offers unique musical and psychological perspectives on one of the most important decisions made in a musician's lifetime: choosing a career. Through stories, anecdotes, research, economic data, personal reflections, and clinical illustrations, she suggests that musicians can be teacher-performers and cultural ambassadors who reach out to others beyond the pandemic as they creatively promote the intrinsic value of music.